You Still Can't Get to Puckum

You Still Can't Get to Puckum

more folks and tales from Delmarva

Hal Roth

Nanticoke Books

Vienna, Maryland

Manufactured in the United States of America by Victor Graphics

ISBN 0-9647694-4-1

Published by Nanticoke Books, Vienna, Maryland

First Edition—June, 2000

Other Books by Hal Roth:

Conversations in a Country Store
Reminiscing on Maryland's Eastern Shore (1995)

You Can't Never Get to Puckum
Folks and Tales from Delmarva (1997)

The Monster's Handsome Face
Patty Cannon in Fiction and Fact (1998)

The Entailed Hat by George Alfred Townsend
Edited and Illustrated by Hal Roth (2000)

For my sister, Pat

Contents

In addition to the titled stories or small collections listed opposite, short, sometimes edited anecdotes as told to the author appear on the following pages: 8, 37, 45, 68, 76, 91, 104, 114, 121, 130, 138, 154, 162, 163, 172, 179, 180, 188, 189, 196, 213, 227, and 228.

Illustrations

The cover photograph was taken on Chicone Road in Dorchester County, Maryland.

The photographs of Robert W. Messenger are owned by Robin Jameson and Miriam Thomas and were copied with permission by Hal Roth.

The Messenger cannery and Eagle Mills pictures were borrowed from the 1904 *History of Federalsburg.*

Hal and Margaret Roth were photographed by using a self timer.

Ed. Okonowicz in the Welsh Tract Graveyard is the work of Jack Buxbaum.

Brice Stump made the image of the author and Patty Cannon's skull to illustrate a story by Brice Stump in *The* (Salisbury, Maryland) *Daily Times.*

All other photographs were taken by the author.

Acknowledgments

Most of the titled stories included in this volume have been published in *Tidewater Times*, some in a slightly altered form or under a different name. My thanks to Publisher David Pulzone and Editor Anne Farwell for the freedom they allow me in choosing subjects for my monthly feature.

Parts of "Return of the Trumpeters" appeared in two separate commentaries in *The* (Cambridge, Maryland) *Daily Banner*, and I thank Terry White for those opportunities.

"The Ghost of Cannon Hall" and "Patty Cannon's Skull" are reprinted with some modification from *The Monster's Handsome Face—Patty Cannon in Fiction and Fact*, Hal Roth, Nanticoke Books, 1998.

Books are rarely the product of a single individual. I am grateful to the following for an enormous variety of contributions to this one: Jean Andrew, John Andrew, Danielle Bellezza, Mary Bellezza, Paul Bellezza, Marilee Bradley, Merton Bradley, Dallas Bradshaw, Everett Bradshaw, R. Lee Burton, Jack Buxbaum, the late Billy Carneal, Robert Christopher, Dr. Alvin Coleman, the late Beulah Dodson, Bill Eberspacher, Bill Evans, Bob Evans, Robert Ferris, Chief Sewell Winterhawk Fitzhugh, Amy Fooks, Lloyd Fooks, the late Nora Foxwell, Warren Foxwell, Lisa Jo Frech, Claude Gootee, John Edward Goslee, A. V. Griffies, Jeff Griffies, Marilyn Griffies, John Groton, Bill Hammond, the late Lee Harper, Marty Harper, Susan Hartman, V. K. Holtzendorf, John Root Hopkins, Allen Hurley, Granville Hurst, Robin Jameson, Beth Kennedy, Jack Knowles, William Langfitt, Roland Layton, Arthur Little, Janice Marshall, Bonnie Maull, Lyal Merriken, Donald Messenger, Lynn Messenger, Bernard Murphy, Wade Murphy, Ed Okonowicz, Michelle O'Malley, Tim Pritchett, the late Harold Richardson, Donielle Rininger, the other Hal Roth, Cathy Ruark, Tami Schmidt, the late Dr. Jerry Shields, Gavin Shire, Jimmy Simmons, Chris Slaughter, Sam Smith, Judge Marvin Smith, Carole Spicer, Jim Spicer, Brice Stump, Miriam Thomas, "Peanut" Tingle, the late Winfield Trice, June Truitt, David Warfield, Eddie West, Bob Wetherall, Gary White, Tom Wisner, and the late Glenn Wilson. I apologize to those left out, whose names I have forgotten or failed to ask.

Some of the writers who have influenced passages herein are mentioned throughout the text; others are not. They include: George Carey, Charles B. Clark, Hulbert Footner, Ellenor Merriken, Raphael Semmes, Donald Shomette, John H. K. Shannahan, George Alfred Townsend, Adam Wallace, and William Warner.

Finally, I am indebted to Elsie Smith, who took time from her very busy schedule to read the text and assist me in identifying errors and considering other points of view.

Introduction

Delmarva is that peninsula extending like a burly appendage from the southeastern corner of Pennsylvania, its shores washed on the west by Chesapeake Bay and on the east by the Delaware River, Delaware Bay, and the Atlantic Ocean. It incorporates all three counties of Delaware, nine of Maryland's twenty-three, and two which appear to have strayed from the mainland of Virginia. **DELMARVA—DEL**aware, **MAR**yland, **Vir**gini**A**. Both geographically and economically it would have made far more sense if the whole of the peninsula had been merged into a single state. Eastern Shoremen, as Delmarva Marylanders call themselves, have at times seriously suggested secession from the western shore, and, on at least one occasion, Virginia has absentmindedly excluded Accomack and Northampton Counties from a state map.

Some divide the peninsula's history into two periods: the years before the bridge and those after. "The bridge" is the William Preston Lane Memorial Bridge, more commonly referred to as the "Bay Bridge." First opened to traffic in 1952, it links Sandy Point on Maryland's Western Shore with Kent Island on Delmarva. Before the bridge, access to the peninsula was either by way of the northern neck or across the watery expanse of the Chesapeake. Few bothered. As a result of their isolation and privation, it is little wonder that Delmarvians developed a self-reliant and individualistic culture and have sometimes been labeled fiercely independent.

But the twin spans of steel and concrete have brought great changes to Delmarva, and, historically speaking, the transformation has been rapid. "Come heres," as Shoremen sometimes refer to those who have migrated to the peninsula, are beginning to outnumber "from heres," and in another generation most first-person links to the times before the bridge will have been lost. With *Conversations In A Country Store*,

You Can't Never Get To Puckum, and now in *You Still Can't Get to Puckum*, I have been attempting to preserve a few of the more obscure events of Delmarva's history, its lore, its characters—old and new—and to poke a little fun here and there at that political bunch on the other shore.

Longer stories are told in my own voice, though I use a large number of quotations from my sources. In the shorter, untitled tales, every attempt has been made to be as true as possible to the speech of those who shared the narrative with me. Sometimes a story, as presented, may be a composite constructed from the versions of several individuals or from several tellings.

I invite all of you who read these pages to share *your* stories with me and perhaps have them included in future books. You can contact me by sending a note to Nanticoke Books, Box 333, Vienna, Maryland 21869, or look for me in the phone book. But please double check before calling so you don't bother the other Hal Roth (see page 105).

Hal Roth
Vienna, Maryland
April, 2000

You Still Can't Get
To Puckum

I had passed the sign dozens of times, always wondering what lay down Puckum Road. One day I made the turn and discovered only a few scattered houses and a tract of cut-over woods before the thoroughfare terminated at its juncture with Wesley Road. On my way home I stopped at a country store and inquired about Puckum.

"You can't never get to Puckum," the proprietor replied. "No sir! You start down Puckum Road, and you ask where it's at, and they tell you to keep on down the road. After a while you stop and ask again, and they tell you to just keep down the road. Finally—you ain't never got there, but the next time you stop to find out where you at, you done passed it. It's a fact; you can't never get to Puckum."

That wonderful response launched me on a fun-filled quest for what may turn out to be Delmarva's version of Brigadoon and resulted in "You Can't Never Get To Puckum," an article which later became the title story for a collection of tales about the peninsula.

The day after the story first appeared in a local newspaper, I encountered an elderly gentleman in the post office.

"I seen you in the paper yesterday," he greeted me.

"Well, let me ask you, then," I smiled, "have *you* ever been to Puckum?"

"Maybe I come to Puckum one time," he replied, "but I didn't know I was there. Maybe I just kept on goin', see." And with that brief retort he tucked his mail under his arm and kept on going.

A day later I talked with Lee Harper, who shared a wonderful family legend about Blackbeard having once sailed his forty-gun sloop, *Queen Anne's Revenge*, up the Nanticoke River and into the Northwest Branch. According to Lee, all the Harpers thereabouts are descended from a sailor who jumped ship while the infamous pirate spent a winter anchored in Puckum Creek, out of harm's way.

While the "Thicket of Puckum" or "Puckum Flats," as many old timers refer to the region, is frequently described as lying along the northeast bank of Marshyhope Creek and entirely within the boundaries of Dorchester County, that may not always have been the case. In *The Entailed Hat*, a novel by George Alfred Townsend about the life and times of Patty Cannon and her nefarious gang of kidnappers and murderers, we find the following reference to Puckum: "They call the country around Crotcher's [Crotcher's Ferry—now Brookview] Wire Neck, caze no neck is left that kin be twisted off; the country in lower Car'line they calls 'Puckem,' caze the crops is so puckered up."

The only geographical references to the name which I have been able to find on maps of any period are Puckum Road and Puckum Creek, the former crossing the latter a short distance west of the settlement of Eldorado, all well within the boundaries of Dorchester.

Whenever I encounter someone whom I feel will have an opinion, I ask, "How do you get to Puckum?" The replies have encompassed a lot of geography.

"From Hurlock you go across the Harrison Ferry Bridge. On the other side of the bridge you take the first right. You go down a-ways and come to a road that goes to the right. That's Puckum Road. Take a right, and that's Puckum."

These directions, provided by a Hurlock resident, place you squarely at the intersection of Puckum Road and Puckum Creek, but other opinions are numerous:

"Puckum," one woman informed me, "starts on the other side of the Harrison Ferry Bridge [from Hurlock] and runs all the way to Delaware. Patty Cannon was included in Puckum."

Another lady insisted, "It starts at Federalsburg and runs all along the river [Marshyhope Creek] to Eldorado."

A lot of people refer to Finchville as Puckum.

"I lived in Finchville when I was a child, and they called it Puckum back then. To people who have lived there for several generations, Finchville and Puckum are one and the same. The men say Puckum; the women say Finchville."

"Puckum is like Finchville. Outside of Federalsburg they put up a sign pointing you to Finchville, and that's the last you ever see or hear tell of it. And there's no sign at all for Puckum."

"My father always said he lived in the capitol of Puckum; that's Finchville."

One gentleman emphatically told me, "I don't know how to tell you to get to Puckum, but I know it when I'm there."

"I'll tell you where I always understood it was," another expounded, "and where I understood it was, ain't where everybody else says it is. The minute you turn down that Puckum Road [in Eldorado] you turn left. Back where that little pond is, it was a settlement of some kind back there. It was down that road, that's all I know, and I never asked no questions."

"Puckum is on the Sharptown Road [Maryland Route 313]. You know where the police camp is? Well, it's right next to that camp."

"Puckum is up toward Preston. There used to be a Puckum Road up there somewhere, and the Indians had a town there called Puckum."

"It's where Bobby lived when he was alive—Eldorado. They always called him the mayor of Puckum."

"My grandparents used to talk about Puckum. It was just down there somewhere out of the way."

"I can't tell you where Puckum is. Seventy to eighty years ago, already, people didn't quite know where Puckum was."

"I don't think Puckum is any definitive place. The reason it's nebulous—if you go into Indian lore, it's where their hunting ground was. They just shifted around, and so Puckum doesn't have a border."

In *Herring Hill*, the late Ellenor Merriken's delightful anecdotal history of Federalsburg, she credits an Indian chief named Puckham as the source of the name and describes the center of his village as having been located on the banks of the Marshyhope about four miles below Federalsburg, but I have been unable to document this claim.

"Old John Colbourne knew where Chief Puckum was buried," Lyal Merriken told me, but John is gone and does not seem to have left specific directions to any grave site.

Whether Chief Puckham and John Puckham, a Monie Indian who married a free black woman in Somerset County and moved, some say, to Dorchester to escape social persecution, are one and the same, I have not been able to determine. John Puckham's marriage to Jone Johnson is verifiable; his persecution and relocation to Dorchester have yet to be proved.

For some reason Puckum gained an other-side-of-the-track status over the years. "It was just an out-of-the-way place," one gentleman volunteered. "Nobody wanted to admit they lived there."

Jimmy Simmons told me that his brother telephoned their mother one day when he was on the road and said, "Mom, do you remember when we got on your nerves, how you used to tell us you wished we were in Puckum? Well, I'm in Puckum, and I just thought I'd call and tell you."

Another lower Dorchester resident remembered that when he and his siblings were misbehaving, his mother would often mutter, "I'd rather be in Puckum."

"Even now," another county native offered, "that Fork District is sort of not in the rest of Maryland. You're just ignored up in that area."

But times are changing. I met one woman who proudly informed me that she had spent her honeymoon in Puckum, although we agreed that Niagara Falls is probably in no danger of losing its traditional fame as a destination for newly-weds.

"I live in Puckum," is a confession which lately seems to almost attach some prestige, and I like to think that I may have had something to do with that. June Truitt mused that if everyone who now claims Puckum as their residence or former residence was for real, the place would be bigger than Baltimore City.

At a book signing I became aware of a man staring at the cover of *You Can't Never Get to Puckum* with a mixed look of fascination and disbelief that such a book could exist. Tim Pritchett introduced himself as "one of the original Puckum hell raisers."

"A lot of people in Puckum don't have much to do," Tim explained. "We all worked on chicken farms. When I was ten years old, I worked on the weekends, and at that time I got paid two dozen double-yolked eggs a week. Some of us took a bunch of our eggs one night and started bombing cars, and it so happened that the car we got the best hit on was a police car. He chased us down, and holding one boy by the collar, the trooper said, 'You're nothin' but a bunch of Puckum hell raisers.' So ever since then we live by that name. I left there twenty years ago, but there's no way I can shake it."

Using Maryland Route 313 as a centerline, Tim describes Puckum as the area which connects Puckum Road to Finchville and Shady Rest and Allen's Corner.

"That's us," he beamed, clearly pleased with his Puckum heritage.

R. Lee Burton, author of *Canneries of the Eastern Shore*, reminded me of another traditional Puckum industry when he sent a vegetable picker's chit which reads: "Charles Marine, One Unit, Puckum Acres."

"From an old song," Lee's note read: "Now there's a place called Do-wa-ditty/It ain't no town and it ain't no city/But that's what I like about the South," and then went on to offer: "Now there's a Dorchester place called Puckum/But there's a catch; it may be a patch/Just what it really may be is a puzz-lum," to which he added, "Umm, it needs some work. I pass the baton."

Jonathan Stoddard claims a rather subjective view of Puck-um. In a letter from his Virginia home he reminisced: "I was born in Manse Rehoboth [in Eldorado] in the great blizzard of January-February, 1922. The storm prevented my grandfather, Francis R. Breuil, from getting my mother to the hospital in Cambridge. The general practitioner rode in by horseback from Hurlock, arriving after I was born with the assistance of a black midwife who lived in a shack down by the branch. Even with the onset of senility I have little trouble remembering my birth date—2/2/22."

While we sat at his dining room table, John Andrew pre-sented me with a rare glimpse of life in Puckum earlier in the twentieth century: "My first job," Andrew recalled, "was work-ing for Southern States for Roy Merriken. I'd start out in the mornin' with five ton of feed and bring back several cases of hatchin' eggs. I put in fifty hours a week for twelve dollars.

"I'd get to Elwood Brinsfield's station to get a cheese sand-wich, and there'd be a guy I'd have to pitch horseshoes with and let him beat me. Then, if I was lucky, I could get on with it.

"I'd get to one place, and a farmer would be takin' his nap in bib overalls.

"'You dumb boy, you're breakin' up my nap. Don't you know I take a nap after lunch. You're no good anyway, and I'm not gonna pay you today.'

"I'd say, 'OK, don't pay me. I'll go down to the barn and get your feed and put it back on the truck.' I always had to stack the feed where everybody wanted it—hundred pound bags, you know.

"'Wait a minute, Daisey's got a cup of coffee for you.'

"They all knew I drank coffee, and a lot of 'em had coffee made. I'd come back, and he'd be countin' out the cash for me. I'd say, 'Whew, you saved me that time.'

"'You're still no good,' he'd say.

"One day the man said, 'Johnnie's out there workin' by hisself—goin' to Baltimore with a load of watermelons, and old as I am, I gotta help him.' He said, 'I'd give somethin' purty if I could have a man could throw them watermelons up there to Johnny. You wouldn't do nothin' like that, would you?'

"I said, 'Miss Daisy, you got another cup of coffee?'

"He said, 'Darn right she does.'

"I said, 'OK.'

"I went out about an hour and throwed up a load of watermelons to his son, and he took off to Baltimore.

"I unloaded some feed corn for another old gentleman, and he said, 'You're just the man I want.' He was rentin' a place to another fellow, and he said, 'I need to move that guy. I want you to go up there and read this notice to him.'

"I said, 'Whew,' to myself, but I went up and knocked on the door. I was fairly young, you know.

"A real rough guy opened it up and said, 'What do you want?'

"I said, 'I have a notice here; the landlord is going to move you.'

"'Let me see it!'

"I didn't know if he was going to snatch it out of my hand and tear it up or what. He read it and handed it back, and after that he moved.

"This gentleman who was fairly well known down there in Puckum was out coon huntin' one night in the swamp, and evidently he wandered a bit. The game warden got a little notion and got after him. When he caught up with the man, it was just the game warden and this old gentleman. The game warden says, 'Well, I'm gonna hafta carry you in.'

"So the man laid right down on the ground—he was a great big guy—and he says, 'OK, carry me.'

"I don't know exactly what happened, but I think they made peace. The warden never carried him to court anyway.

"They were outstanding people down there, and I loved it—that whole run. They treated me real well, and I was a stranger down there.

"Mrs. Merriken was a businesswoman. She'd give me a bag of money to make change with. I never counted it, and after five years she told me I was thirty-six cents out. I said, 'Well, let me give you the thirty-six cents.'

"'No,' she said, 'it's in your favor.'

"That was what we called the Puckum run, and I never yet found out where Puckum was."

Back in the post office, my octogenarian friend sums it up this way: "I don't think nobody understands about Puckum. You go on up there, and they say, 'Hey, you got to go up a little further.' And after you go up a little further, you got to go up a little further more, and in the end you still ain't never have found it. It's just gone. I imagine Puckum was all gone when they started lookin' for it. You never could get to Puckum, and you still can't get to Puckum."

∞

Old Miles lived down in the Drawbridge area for most of his life. He was an old progger and muskratter and fisherman —anything to make a living.

He had a bunch of boys, and one time he sent 'em out picking tomatoes. That morning they had oatmeal for breakfast, and about the middle of the morning one of them boys got hungry.

He said, "Pop, I can't pick tomatoes on that oatmeal."

"Well, it's a funny thing," Miles said. "If a horse can pull a plow all day long on oats, you oughta be able to pick a few 'maters on 'em."

∞

The Broom Man

I found him quietly at work one scorching July afternoon in the welcome shade of some broad-crowned oak trees on the grounds of the Tuckahoe Steam and Gas Show just north of Easton. The face of his cap announced everything he was likely to offer without being questioned—"Bill's Brooms."

A woman and her husband paused to watch the craftsman's callused fingers thread a stout, red binder cord through the flat of a nearly finished broom. "Do you make these for Acme?" the woman asked. I couldn't decide whether she was serious or joking.

Never raising an eye from his labor, the man in the cap replied, "Nope—Wal-Mart."

Her husband chuckled, and the pair moved on.

The bristling new sweeper was soon completed and racked beside the home-made "broom machine," as William Hammond refers to the assembly of 2X4's and simple metal fixtures. It is the third portable factory he has constructed over the years.

"You ought to sign and number them," I suggested; "then they'd be collector's items, and you could keep count of how many you make."

We chatted for a short while as curious onlookers arrived, gawked for a minute or two, then faded back into the stream of humanity that endlessly flowed among the numerous displays and demonstrations.

"I guess you get a lot of questions and funny comments," I remarked, hoping the Broom Man would share a few with me.

"Well, people run their mouths and go on," Hammond offered, as he arranged a fistful of straw around a new handle. "I told a couple ladies who come up here—they wanted to know how many brooms I made in a year. I said, 'Lord, don't you want me to get no sleep. I ain't got enough time to count how many brooms I make in a year.'"

He folded a fan of straw neatly forward to form the first of what would eventually be several tightly packed layers.

"So they watch awhile," the craftsman continued his story, "and the other one wants to know how long I've been a-makin' brooms. I said, 'Well, I'll tell you, lady, when I was here on the earth before, I made brooms. Then, when I come back here again in 1920 [Hammond was born in 1920], I got my same old job back, and I'm still a-makin' brooms.'

"She looked at me, and she never smiled. She just shook her head and said to the other lady, 'We may just as well go ahead; we ain't gonna get nothin' off'n him.' I get a mess o' stuff like that," he chuckled.

But in spite of his marvelous sense of humor and his frequent public appearances at steam shows, old timers' days, and festivals of all sorts, Bill Hammond is a shy man, not given to initiating conversation with the groups who watch as he meticulously crafts his version of one of the oldest domestic tools known to mankind.

Steam shows, with their large, chatty crowds and their huffing, puffing, chugging machinery and screaming whistles, are no place to conduct an interview, so I arranged to visit with Hammond at his home near Mastens Corner in Delaware.

Retired now after thirty years of performing maintenance and beautification projects for the Delaware highway system, the broom man grew up working on the family farm and in his father's sawmill.

"I didn't go through the eighth grade," he explained. "When I got big enough to ride a ridin' plow, I had to work. You can just as well say all the schoolin' I got was through the winter. When spring come up—on in March—Pop put me on the manure

Bill Hammond at Tuckahoe

spreader, drivin' the team and all that. And later on," he added, "my Uncle Tom had a basket mill, and in the wintertime I went down there [he pronounces there as "thar"] and made baskets—five-eighth baskets. My uncle made everything: sweet potater hampers, berry cups, crates, and all that stuff."

Although his parent's original farm has been reduced to only three acres, Bill Hammond lives in the house where he was born. Since November, 1996, when his wife died, he has lived alone. "I'm lost," he explains simply.

"So tell me how you got started making brooms?" I asked him as he directed me to the garage, which also serves as his shop.

"Charlie Hrupsa got me started," Hammond began to explain. "He lived right over this cornfield," nodding to a field of lush green behind his garage. "He quit farmin', and he sent away and got some broom corn seed. It was comin' on time to plant, and he'd got his ground all ready. He come over here one day, and he says, 'I want you to come up. I got some new corn, and I want you to help me plant it.'

"I looked at that stuff, and I said to him, 'That ain't no corn.'

"'Yes it is,' he said.

"I said, 'It looks like sorghum.'

"'No, it's corn,' he said.

"So anyway, we planted it, and it started to come up. When it got up about three inches, I went over there one day and looked at it. I said, 'Damn Charlie, that's nothin' but that old foxtail grass.'

"Now his daddy had come from the old country and made his own brooms, so Charlie knowed what it was, but he never said a word to me about his daddy makin' brooms.

"Well, it kept on and got up some tall, and the blades begin to look just like corn. Charlie said, 'Well, we got to thin it.' Most of it's suckers, you know. If you thin it down you get better straw. So we went in there and cleaned a mess of it out.

"So it kept on and kept on a-growin', and it started a tassel on top, and the seed and the straw started on there.

"Come on," Hammond said, leading me around to the back of the garage, "and I'll show you."

Behind the garage and outbuildings a large patch of cobless corn stalks confronted us, some of them ten feet tall. At the tops of the sturdy plants, shocks of broom straw were beginning to form. Hammond continued his tale:

"Charlie said, 'I'm gonna make a broom machine, and we're gonna make some brooms.'

"I said, 'Yeah?'

"About the last of August—we'd planted it early—Charlie said, 'I think we'd better get in there and start cuttin' some of that straw.' The seeds were beginnin' to turn a little brown, and you want that straw to stay green.

"Him and I growed straw together till he got so he couldn't do much. It was five or six years we messed and fooled together. I would go to shows with him, and I'd start a broom, and that's all.

"I guess it was about the second year, I asked him if he would help me make a broom machine. He looked at me and laughed. 'It ain't a bit o' need o' doin' it, Billy,' he said; 'you'll never learn how to make a broom.'

"I said, 'Help me make a broom machine, and I'll take it home. The only way I'm gonna start is for me to get to myself.'

"'Ah, you're just gonna give it up,' Charlie said.

"So it went on, and we went to a show one day—I believe it was to Furnace Town. Charlie walked off, so I started this broom on his machine. I was messin' and foolin', and I put two bunches o' straw on there—opposite one to the other—and run my wire around it. I did get that much done, and Charlie come back. He said, 'Damn, you got a couple bunches on there. That'll be the first time.'

"I said, 'Yeah, wasn't nobody around, so I snuck that on there.'

"'Well,' he said, 'that don't look too bad.'

"He messed and fooled there a while, and he hangs out again. When he comes back, then, I had that straw folded and pulled back, and I had the belt on there. I seen him comin', so I quit. Charlie looked at it and laughed. I can see him now. He didn't say a word.

"We was comin' home, and Charlie said, 'Billy, you're gonna have to get in a hurry and go on; I don't see why you can't go ahead.'

"'I'm afraid I'll mess the straw up,' I said. 'You know we don't have much straw.'

"He said, 'Don't worry about that. I can do the same thing.'

"'So are you gonna help me make a broom machine?' I said.

"He never opened his mouth—just come on home. But on Sunday afternoon Charlie come up here, and he said, 'Billy, you get your 2X4's, and I'll help you make a broom machine.'

"Monday night I took them 2X4's up there, and he had the thing all fixed—the barrel and everything all welded up. He took the 2X4's and went on—started makin' it."

Hammond's first machine stands in his shop today, where it is still used to manufacture whisk brooms. He has fabricated two improved models of his own since then. Charlie Hrupsa died years ago, and his broom machine is on display at the Delaware Agriculture Museum in Dover.

"I started with Charlie in '62," Hammond told me, "and went on my own about '65. I still got the first broom I made. I don't show it to many people," he said, as he presented a sturdy, red-handled sweeper for my inspection.

"That looks just fine," I affirmed, but Hammond frowned.

"Looks like a old mule's tail," he said, chuckling.

"Everywhere I go and mention you," I told him, "people say, 'I know him; you can't get a broom anywhere that sweeps better.' Have you ever had a complaint?"

"I had one," he recalled. "I went to a show some years ago, and this lady come up when I wasn't there. She tells my wife: 'I bought a broom from him last year, and it's come to pieces. Will he put the straw back on that handle for me?'

"'He will if he done the work,' my wife says. 'Have you got the broom with you?'

"'I don't live too far from here,' she said; 'I can soon go get it.'

"Sometime in the afternoon, here she come with it. Well, it wasn't my broom. I looked at it, and I says, 'Lady, I didn't make that broom.'

"'O yes you did!' she says.

"'I'll be damned if I did,' I told her; 'that ain't my string.'

"Her face turned red, and she said, 'I bought that broom right here.'

"'If you did,' I told her, 'you didn't buy it from me. But if you want me to put straw on that handle, I'll do it for five dollars.' I was gettin' six dollars for a broom then.

"She walked off and come back in maybe half hour. She says, 'If I was to give you six dollars, would you put straw on that handle?'

"I says, 'Yeah.'

"She give me a dollar more than I asked her. My wife told her: 'It ought to be worth ten—you come and accuse him, and it wasn't his job.'"

I had watched Bill Hammond work at his craft many times over the years and never noticed before that he is missing the first joint of one thumb.

"I was eight years old—it was 1928—and my hand slipped into a fodder cutter," he explained. "The doctor wanted to take this off too." Hammond held up a deformed finger. "I said, 'No, you ain't gonna take that one off.' It was all mashed up, but it ain't too bad.

"I've been lucky around the saw mills and all like that," he continued. "My granddad—all he had was a thumb and a little finger on one hand; the saw just cut everything else right off."

In addition to demonstrating his artisanship at shows all over the Delmarva Peninsula, Bill Hammond installs foundations for manufactured homes.

"Isn't it about time for you to retire again?" I asked him. "Aren't you getting tired of working so hard?"

"Now I'll tell you," he laughed, "I'm gettin' tired, and I may quit, but I'm gonna stay with it as long as I can go. I can't set around, and I can't set still. I pull and haul on cement and stuff like that because I gotta go. I've done it all my life. This mornin' I was up at four-thirty. When I was home on the farm, we had milkin' and all that stuff to do. I've never stopped. I've got to be a-pullin' and a-haulin'. I can't stay in the house. I eat, and I'm up and gone."

∞

Bill Hammond's First Broom

The Devil
on Delmarva

"**M**ost everybody used to carry somethin' to keep the devil off," the old man said. "Mom would tie a charm around my neck. I forget now just what it was, but I guess it worked. I ain't never run up on the devil—not as I know anyway."

In Sunday sermons the devil still plays a prominent role, and his name is invoked with little thought in our everyday conversations—"that poor devil; between the devil and the deep blue sea; a devil of a thing; go to the devil; the devil take the hindmost; give the devil his due; there's gonna be the devil to pay"—but to tell the truth, it's hard to find anybody these days who actually admits to a face to face confrontation with the old fellow. That hasn't always been the case.

For a time the devil was seen flying around Kent County, Maryland. As one gentleman relates the story, "I ain't kiddin' ya'. Everybody with any age on 'em remembers it." The apparition was reported as having "wings just like one of them wingbats," and was also observed sitting on a piling by a creek. "It had people all worried up about it. Some of 'em wouldn't even go outdoor at night."

In Sussex County, Delaware, within sight of the Woodland Ferry, I was told this story about Malihorn—a chief, the woman informed me, of the Nanticoke Indians:

The devil come to old Chief Malihorn one time and told

him that if he wanted to stay here next to the river and plant, he would have to start payin' a tax. The devil said he wanted half the crops. Old Malihorn thought on it for a spell, and finally he said, "Well, let's work it this way: the first year you take the half that grows above the ground, and I take the half that grows below; then the next year we'll change it around." The devil figured that sounded fair, so they shook on it. Come the spring, Malihorn planted potatoes. Come the fall, Malihorn got the potatoes, and the devil got the vines. That riled the devil up right good, but he figured he'd make up for it the next year, and he let it go by. Come next spring, Malihorn planted corn, and the devil, of course, got nothin' but roots. Now that was too much for the old devil, and the two commenced to fussin' and fittin'. They fell right off the bank into this river, and for several days they thrashed up and down that channel, all the way from here to Seaford and back.

I never did learn how the battle ended, but I was informed that because of it there are a number of deep holes even today in the Nanticoke's bottom between Woodland and the Nylon Capitol.

Downstream a few miles, where Marshyhope Creek makes off toward Federalsburg, the tale of Molly Horn and the devil is remembered. I've wondered about the similarity between Malihorn and Molly Horn, and the plot also has a familiar ring, although Molly is reported to have planted potatoes one year and peas and beans instead of corn the next. But Molly had a better right cross than Malihorn, and at the devil's first protest she popped him and sent the evil one skidding across the Dorchester Marshes to the edge of the Chesapeake. When he stood up and shook the mud from his clothing, it fell in a heap around him and formed Devil's Island. Having seen quite enough of Molly, he then dove overboard and created Devil's Hole.

Another version of this tale from the Forks of the Nanticoke pits Mary Ann against the bad one. Their battle in the river resulted in the forty-foot hole at Red Banks. After the devil kicked out the river bottom to form the banks, he carried Mary Ann away.

Getting back to Devil's Island, another legend informs us that a ship bound for the Virginia Shore wrecked on this then uninhabited key. Confronted with seemingly endless marshes and wilderness (probably during mosquito and fly season as well) the stranded passengers declared it to be the realm of the devil, thus providing cartographers with a label to fill the blank space on their maps.

Whatever the origin of the name, the place was called Devil's Island and then Deil's Island for many years. Some writers say that "deil" is a Greek word for devil, while others insist it derives from the Scottish name for Satin. In any event, it is generally accepted that the devil and his works held undisputed sway on all the isles of the Chesapeake for so long that the inhabitants became blinded to their true condition—that is until Joshua Thomas, the famous Methodist parson, began to make the rounds in his dugout canoe to enlighten them. It was about that time, some insist, that the Reverend Dailey changed the names of Devil's Island and the nearby community of Damned Quarter (now Dames Quarter) to alleviate any belief that Satan might have property rights thereabouts. Whatever the stimuli may have been for the changes, the island's name did evolve from Devil's to Deil's,' to Deal's, to Deal. The final revision, a popular story would have us believe, transpired after the postmaster broke the 's off his wooden stamp and never bothered to get a replacement.

Whether you give credence to a devilish connection or not, within about a twenty mile radius of Devil's Island, folklore does record an unusual number of encounters with the Prince of Darkness.

On Smith Island they say the devil made frequent appearances, even disrupting a prayer meeting once. Folks had assembled from every part of the island to hear the words of David Wallace, a preacher from Deal with a voice like thunder, and Hance Lawson, another valiant soldier of the cross from Annamessex. As their exhortations progressed, the house began to shake, and a great anxiety spread among the overflowing crowd. When the wife of the host fell down, crying out for mercy, panic set in. Everyone decided the devil was present and hard after their souls. People began to scatter—some through the windows—and one of them, Zachariah Crockett, ran two miles before he remembered he left his wife behind.

In nearby Crisfield a man named Skidmore consorted with the powers of evil and gained access to a wide range of magical and supernatural powers, perhaps being best remembered for his prowess as a possessed worker. When Skidmore went into the woods to cut firewood, it has been said, you would soon hear the ringing of a dozen axes. If you sought him out, you would find him alone, casually sitting on a stump with dozens of cords of wood stacked around him. "To work like Skidmore" is an expression that lingers to this day in Somerset County. Folklore fails to provide us with any indication as to the eventual fate of Skidmore, but in several other cases we are left with no doubt that souls were collected.

Take the sad legend of George Bender, a resident of Hebron who was addicted to playing the ponies and sold his very substance in exchange for their speed. Friends had noted that whenever George went to the track, he was accompanied by two tall, brawny black men, and the horse of his choice always came in first. Then one afternoon, as a neighbor pointed his skiff toward home from a day's work on the bay, he was startled to encounter George, skipping across the waves in a carriage drawn by two charging black stallions.

"Where are you going, George?" the man shouted to his neighbor.

"I'm off to Hell," came Bender's reply, and when the waterman returned to the dock, he was told that George had passed away that very afternoon.

A Tangier islander named Travis is an even sadder victim, since his eternal damnation resulted from an inability to find enough work to provide for his family. One night as Travis sat by the fire agonizing over his failures, a stranger entered the room and invited him to a meeting at Job's Cove the following midnight. There he would learn how to acquire whatever material goods he wished. Travis went and was told by the devil to bury two pennies, an act which sealed their contract. Although Travis prospered beyond his wildest dreams, the time eventually came when his family was gathered around his deathbed. Just then a stranger appeared, swept the old man up in his arms, and carried him off. Everyone knew it was the devil, and they didn't even bother to have a funeral.

While the outcome of almost any pact with Satin was inevitable, at least Bender and Travis were able to divert it for a natural lifetime of success. A fellow down in the Neck District of Dorchester County, however, learned the hard way not to mess around with Old Nick while the game was playing out. This chap, whose name I have never learned, had let it be known that he would willingly trade his soul for some gold. One evening a stranger appeared and told him to hang his boots upright against the wall before he retired that night. When he awoke the following morning, the boots were filled with gold coins. Soon afterward, when he again decided he was in need, the act was repeated with the same reward. You can imagine how it went: the boots were hung more and more frequently until the greedy chap finally decided one night to cut out the toes. Off to bed he went, wringing his hands in anticipation. Like a kid on Christmas morning, he couldn't wait to go downstairs, and when he did, his wildest expectations were met: the room was filled with gold piled as high as the boots had been hung. But like I said, it's best not to mess with Old Scratch. Before he could shovel the gold into bags, the stranger appeared and carried him off, never to be seen again.

Those who refused to be tempted, however, had little trouble avoiding damnation. On a marshy island north of Tangier, the devil appeared to Miss Christy in the form of a small black bull. Since there wasn't a single bull on all of Shanks at that time, she knew right away it had to be the devil. "Go away, devil," she said, "I don't want nothin' to do with you," and the little bull evaporated into thin air.

He tried Lloyd McCready too. "I'd been over to Wards Crossin'," McCready claimed, "and was comin' home about midnight, when I seen this fire in a ditch. I had my revolver, so I went over there to take a look at it. All of a sudden I heard these chains a-rattlin', and I knew right off it was the devil. I lit out o' there and run all the way home. Next day I went back and seen a deck o' cards scattered all around that ditch, tore up in a thousand little pieces. I knowed then for sure it was the devil. They always did say that he's in the cards."

Some might wonder, what with the devil hanging around so much, just how far hell is from Delmarva. Not very, if you take any stock in Calvert McCready's dream.

"They called him Captain Cal," the old fellow who told me the story began, "and he lived just about to Henry's Crossroads. He was a very religious old man—a nice old fellow. He had a dream one time, and he dreamed that he wanted to start a match factory, and he went to hell to get a load of brimstone. He claimed that Captain Frank Oliphant and Captain Dick Marshall went with him. He said they left from around Crossroads on a Friday evenin' with a oxcart, and they went on down that road, and they got there on Sunday mornin'. Somebody said to him, 'Well, if you left on Friday evening on a oxcart and got there on Sunday morning, hell can't be all that far then.' Captain Cal said, 'No, I figure it must be down about Elliott's Island somewhere.'"

To which a resident of Elliott replied, "The devil you say!"

∞

The Captain is a Lady

A few miles above Sharptown, shortly after crossing into Delaware and past the mouth of Broad Creek, boaters need beware of a cable on which a motorized scow regularly chugs back and forth between the shores of the Nanticoke River. Operated without charge by the State of Delaware, the Woodland Ferry has a capacity of three passenger vehicles and boasts a service among the longest in the nation.

At one time this tranquil river crossing and small collection of tidy homes were known as Cannon's Port and later as Cannon's Ferry, borrowing the name of the area's first settler, James Cannon (1661-1711), who arrived in Dorchester in the Province of Maryland sometime before August 4, 1683, the date on which he signed John Taylor's will as a witness.

In what was then known as Nanticoke Forest, the first of Cannon's several land grants and purchases on the north bank of the river was surveyed for him on June 28, 1688, a year after the Nanticoke Indian Chief Ahopperoon renewed the peace made between his brother, Vinnacakossimon, and Lord Baltimore in 1678. James built his plantation home, a wharf, and a tobacco curing house a short distance down river from the mouth of Muddy Creek and cleared land to plant the "divine herb," which became his chief crop.

While there is evidence that he used dugout canoes, forerunner of the Chesapeake bugeye, for river commerce, often securing two of them side by side to carry hogsheads of tobacco, I have found no testimony to suggest that James ever main-

tained a ferry. The earliest documentation I have seen to suggest the antiquity of that enterprise is a statement in court records at "Snowhill Town," Worcester County, Maryland, which
is dated November 4, 1766, and states that 1500 pounds of tobacco were paid to Jacob Cannon "for keeping a ferry over Nanticoke River the year past." Jacob was a grandson of James.

To eliminate confusion which might be caused by references to both Maryland and Delaware, we need to understand
that Cannon's Ferry once traversed the Nanticoke River between the Maryland counties of Dorchester and Worcester, but
ratification of the Mason-Dixon Line in 1769 placed it within
the boundaries of Pennsylvania. Finally, it was claimed by
Delaware when that state's government was established in 17-
76. So in a span of only seven years the Cannon enterprises,
without moving, operated under the jurisdiction of three different colonies or states.

Upon Jacob Cannon's death in 1780, his son Isaac, then ten
years of age, was willed all his father's lands, housing, water-
craft, and one mare. Isaac's brother, Jacob, would be born
later that year. While her sons were growing up, the widow
Betty Cannon continued the business of the port and ferry.

After the Cannons had incurred the high expense of con-
structing a causeway across the marsh and a road to Broad
Creek, several other individuals moved scows to the site and
began to ferry passengers at lower rates than the Cannons
could afford to charge. Betty petitioned the Delaware Legislature for relief, and on February 2, 1793, that body granted to
Betty and Isaac Cannon the "sole and exclusive" privilege of
operating a ferry across the Nanticoke River for fourteen years.
The grant was renewed in spite of the fact that travelers were
often obliged, as one written complaint stated, "to wait in the
cold and rain and snow for hours before we can wake or rouse
with a loud strong voice or conk shell an old Negro slave upwards of sixty years of age, who has been the only ferryman to
manage and row a scow."

Isaac and Jacob Cannon were shrewd businessmen who

eventually amassed an estate of nearly 5,500 acres of land in Maryland and Delaware, including many houses, stores, warehouses, factories, slaves, and a fleet of vessels, but their uncompromising methods of conducting business made enemies and perhaps resulted in Jacob's murder.

When Jacob accused Owen O'Day, a former henchman to Patty Cannon, of stealing a bee gum from one of his farms, an argument ensued. O'Day shot Jacob Cannon on the ferry wharf in April, 1843, as Jacob was returning from a visit to the governor, to whom he had appealed for protection from threatened assaults. He succumbed to his wound a few days later, and Isaac died from undisclosed causes a month afterwards.

Should you visit Woodland and pause at the ferry house to read the Delaware historical marker displayed there, be aware that it contains several errors: 1793 was the year in which the Delaware Legislature granted exclusive rights to the Cannons to operate a ferry at this location, not the inaugural year for that operation. We have seen that the ferry had been established by 1766 and perhaps earlier. And, secondly, Isaac Cannon was not Betty's husband as the marker claims; he was her son. The Cannons rest in brick vaults beneath heavy capstones only a few dozen yards to the southwest of the marker. The location of Betty's husband Jacob's grave is not known.

I was returning from a trip to Dover one afternoon and decided to take the scenic route home by crossing the Nanticoke on the ferry. When I arrived at the river opposite Woodland, the conveyance was in mid-stream churning toward me. A few minutes later I eased my van up the ramp, pulled ahead to the barrier, and got out to stretch my legs.

"Sure is a hot one," I remarked to the deck hand.

"It's summertime," he replied in a tone which clearly inferred, "What else would you expect in August on Delmarva?"

I refused to be put down.

"Not bad here on deck, but I'll bet he's steaming up there," as I nodded toward the skipper's perch.

The young man looked at me as though my intellectual deficiencies were more than he could ever hope to overcome on a hundred-yard voyage. "The captain," he said, "is a lady!"

I glanced at the pilot house for the first time, and, indeed, my informer was correct; the individual at the throttle, conspicuous in a bright orange shirt, was a lady. As she gently eased the scow into its berth on the Woodland shore, I caught her eye, and we exchanged smiles.

The next time I saw Captain Bonnie Maull was on an unusually warm December day. The temperature had risen to the mid seventies, and the Nanticoke shimmered under a hazy afternoon sun. When I parked my van and walked on board, I did not realize that the ferry was operating without its cable. She was free-floating, and the tide was in flood.

The scow has no rudder for steering and depends entirely upon its cable for guidance. But the vessel does have twin props, and if the wind and tide are not too strong, a skillful skipper can control her by manipulation of the throttles. I watched with admiration as Captain Bonnie finessed the bulky craft across to the Laurel side and threaded the ramp slot like a needle.

"You're pretty good at that," I complimented her.

"I've had a lot of experience," she countered modestly, then added, "I hate to close it. People depend on it."

I told her the story of my August ride and her mate's response—"The captain is a lady!"—to my use of the masculine pronoun.

"Sometimes they wouldn't think so," she grinned in response.

"Oh, how's that?" I probed.

"Sometimes you have to go to trucker talk, if that's all they understand," Captain Bonnie replied, and then told the story I was hoping for.

"For the longest time I was the only female working outside in Sussex County—what they call the orange shirts. It was the good old boys' club, you know. One fellow got right bad. I finally said, 'Listen, I think I'll have to explain it to you in trucker's talk.' And so I explained it! When I got through, he understood exactly what I meant."

The radio crackled with the voice of a tugboat captain, letting us know he would be passing through in a few minutes, inbound with two loaded stone barges for Seaford.

"A barge broke away once coming this way," Captain Bonnie remembered. "He called me when he was coming around the bend. He said, 'I've got one loose, but don't worry, I'm gonna run her up in the marsh.' And that's what he did." Trauma to the shore from the grounding is still evident below Woodland.

"Have there been any accidents with the tugs?" I wanted to know.

"The man I replaced. The ferry was sitting in the slip, and a tug came too close to the shore. If they come too close, they'll pick up the cable. The tug hooked the cable and pulled the ferry out and threw the captain out of the pilot house and down on the deck. He broke his back and is crippled for the rest of his life. When the tide is extremely low and a tug is coming through, I won't let cars on, and I get off," the skipper said.

"I imagine the cable has caused some other accidents with pleasure boaters," I observed.

"I've seen three beautiful boats get torn up bad. They don't pay any attention to the light or to us in here blowing the horn. One was a $70-75,000 boat, and it had over $10,000 in damage. It was an inboard, and he came over the top of the cable. It stopped him and threw him like a slingshot. Another time the lights were flashing and boats were here waiting, and he just came on through. The rider was thrown out, and it tore the whole transom and everything out of the boat. They're always hitting the cable, but most of the time they just nick it."

Captain Bonnie was not on duty the night two drunks took their last ferry ride. After rowdy and dangerous behavior by the men on a first crossing, that captain denied them access when they returned later. Furious, the inebriated driver stomped the accelerator to the floor, crashed the vehicle through the net barrier, traversed the short length of the vessel, and, failing to stop, propelled himself and his passenger into the channel of the Nanticoke. Neither survived.

Again I expressed my amazement at the skill with which the captain maneuvered the boat against the tide with only the use of opposing props.

Captain Bonnie shrugged off my compliments, "I could do this blindfolded," she remarked casually.

A small cabin cruiser came into view downstream, and its captain, obviously a regular on the river, called in on his radio.

"Yes, sir, I was waiting for you," Captain Bonnie replied. "It's a beautiful day. I've been wondering why you haven't been through. I don't have a cable, so there won't be any lights."

"You don't have a cable?" the voice responded incredulously.

"No, I'm free-wheeling."

"You're not going to go back and forth without a cable?"

"Yes, sir, I am."

"If you keep that up, they're not going to put the cable back on."

"I wish they'd give me a rudder and a steering wheel so I could go somewhere," the captain teased.

As we chugged back and forth across the placid Nanticoke, transporting several vehicles and their passengers on each run, I commented about a single fisherman casting from the Laurel shore.

"He's here at least once a month," the lady in the orange shirt remarked, "and he's so patient. And there's a couple that comes to catch catfish—I'm surprised they're not here today. She baits his hook and everything. He won't even take the fish off the hook. Then she catches two at a time. She always beats him."

The engines whirred and roared as Captain Bonnie alternated between them to maneuver into the slip.

"Well," I said as I backed down the stairway of the pilot house, "after watching you operate without a cable, I'm going to write to DELDOT when I get home and recommend they promote you from captain to admiral."

Captain Bonnie Maull on the Woodland Ferry

"I'd appreciate that," Captain Bonnie grinned.

Shortly after our chat I was driving through Woodland one afternoon and noticed Captain Bonnie in the pilot house. On the spur of the moment I decided to try and rattle her a little—I should have known better.

Turning on my VHF radio, I set it to channel 13—the ferry frequency—and depressed the call button: "This is Task Force Delta to Woodland Ferry."

"This is Woodland Ferry; go ahead."

I set my jaw and continued in what I hoped would be a convincing military manner: "Hello Woodland. This is commander Hooper. I have a light cruiser and two destroyers inbound for Seaford, ETA Woodland, oh, about 14:50. I'm drawing three fathoms. Do you have any special instructions on clearance?"

"Not a bit," came the nonplused reply.

"Can you pull your scow up on shore till we clear?"

After a very few seconds of silence, Captain Bonnie snapped, "Just come aboard," her tone dripping with sarcasm.

"Is that negative or affirmative Woodland?"

Another pause, then, "Have you had a little Christmas cheer?" This time I could "hear" a smile in the voice.

"I understand you know trucker talk, Captain. Is that anything like sailor talk?"

(Laughter)

"I thought I might get a little trucker talk out of you."

"Not on the radio."

"You're no fun."

"I know it."

I should have remembered what I had been told the day I first met her: "The captain is a lady!"

∞

The Crapo Papers

History is a funny thing. I mean that, of course, not in the literal sense but as a way of saying that you can't believe everything you read. For a variety of personal and political reasons—frequently for profit, often for vagaries quickly forgotten—matters of history have repeatedly been slanted.

Take Christopher Columbus as an example. Few individuals occupy a more visible and seemingly secure place in American History. Since the birthdays of George Washington and Abraham Lincoln have been combined as Presidents' Day, Columbus is one of only two people with national holidays honoring their name. Everyone knows the year he discovered America. Who hasn't recited as a child: "In 1492, Columbus sailed the ocean blue?" Our history is even divided into two parts: pre-Columbian and everything since.

I don't have the space here to go into the details, but almost everything we "know" about Columbus from tradition and from our history books is either false or unverifiable. The most obvious error is the belief that Columbus was the first man to discover America, a premise which ignores the fact that people from other continents had reached the Americas many times before 1492. In truth, Columbus might more accurately be called the last man to discover America.

Another of the great American myths is the story of the first Thanksgiving and the general belief that the Pilgrims, the men and women of the Plymouth Colony who arrived on our shores in 1620, were America's first settlers. Why do so many ignore the obvious? Those whom we know as Native Americans, nomads who crossed the Bering Straits before anyone else even suspected this half of the world existed, had populated nearly the entire western hemisphere thousands of years before Columbus and the Pilgrims were born.

We have also largely failed to remember and credit the 1526 settlement in what is now South Carolina and the Spanish colonists who later abandoned their African slaves to the southeastern wilderness when they left? Why do we not acknowledge these pioneers, especially their discarded slaves, who must have had a far more difficult time than the Pilgrims ever dreamed of?

And why do we ignore the French Protestants who settled St. Augustine, Florida, only to be massacred by the Spanish forces who established their own fort there in 1526. Spanish priests, adventurers, and settlers had also migrated into parts of several western states long before the Pilgrims landed.

Even the Chesapeake Bay was settled and explored before Massachusetts. Anyone who has completed a course in United States history should recall that the first permanent English settlement was established at Jamestown in 1607, and by 1608 John Smith had explored and mapped the entire bay area.

Although William Claiborne, a renegade trader from Virginia, had established an outpost on the Eastern Shore some years earlier, Maryland's first official English residents arrived in 1634 and located on the St. Mary's River, a tributary of the Potomac.

Knowledge about Maryland's early days took a giant leap recently, when a descendant of one of John Henry's servants came across a trunk filled with parchments and letters and a great variety of other documents in an attic in Crapo, Maryland. Henry, you will remember, was a prominent Eastern Shore planter and merchant and one of the state's early governors after the original proprietary colony became a state.

These chronicles, which the Library of Congress has collectively labeled the "Crapo (pronounce that 'Cray-po' please) Papers," reveal some interesting and previously unknown facts about the Calvert family's dream for its colony. Also found were memorandums which contain shocking details of a Western Shore conspiracy against the Calverts and the original settlers of Delmarva.

The Crapo Papers contain references which clearly outline Cecil Calvert's intentions to develop the Eastern Shore, with its pleasing geography, incomparable soils, and moderate climate, as the political and cultural center for his colony. Cecil Calvert was the second Lord Baltimore.

While we are aware of earlier documentary evidence suggesting that Lord Baltimore intended to establish Maryland's chief city—a metropolis honoring his family title—on the shores of Delmarva's Nanticoke River, the newly discovered archives detail much more of the story than has heretofore been revealed.

A large tract of land was surveyed and cleared in a sheltered area on the northwest bank of that placid, unspoiled river, which John Smith had originally labeled the "Cuskarawaok." Archaeological evidence as well as native tradition suggests that the site, known as Emperor's Landing to the Nanticoke Indians, had probably been occupied by Native Americans for hundreds of years.

But development was not destined to progress smoothly for the fledgling city of Baltimore. As so often happens when there is wealth and power at stake, enemies quickly launched an attempt to deflect Lord Baltimore's plans.

The most notable among Cecil Calvert's detractors, the Crapo Papers show, was a lesser nobleman who had been forced to flee England because of irrational behavior while serving in Parliament. After his arrival in America, the egotistical Lord Schaefer, who was known on occasion to dress in weird costumes and post threatening letters to citizens, established a trading post on the Patapsco River and began to refer to the Eastern Shore as the outhouse of the colony.

Years afterward, one of Lord Schaefer's descendants was elected governor of the state and—true to his genes—carried on the family tradition of irresponsible behavior in office.

Several other conspirators, among them a defecting Susque-hannock warrior named Ketchacarp, were determined that de-velopment should be concentrated on the Western Shore, where their consortium had speculated heavily in prime waterfront and industrially zoned property.

For a while the tug of war between these two groups was a standoff. Lord Baltimore gained some breathing space for a few months when a conflict arose within the ranks of the plotters, who had by now incorporated as "The Western Shore Alliance to Suppress the Eastern Shore."

Ketchacarp, who in his youth had made war on colonists and other tribes of Indians with equal ferocity, had come, the Crapo Papers clearly illustrate, to see the handwriting on the wall. He sensed that the Europeans were on the land to stay, and Ketchacarp hoped, through his pledge of near filial devo-tion to the wealthy Englishmen, to save a piece of his family's ancestral hunting grounds for himself and eventually gain con-cessions to establish casinos at the head of the bay.

But Ketchacarp's days were numbered. The internal friction reached fever pitch when one of the highrollers named Glen-dening, younger son of Prince George, swore that no gambling would ever be permitted by Indians as long as he had a breath left in his body. Gambling, insisted Glendening, was a privi-lege to be reserved for chiefs.

Ketchacarp eventually slipped away to the north with a band of his former enemies, the Nanticoke, who were rapidly being displaced from the Eastern Shore by Lord Baltimore's plan-ning and zoning commission; and today, after wandering the country for fifteen generations, Ketchacarp's descendants are wealthy casino owners in Massachusetts, California, Nevada, and North Dakota.

The plottings against Calvert and the Eastern Shore be-came very complicated, and further study of the Crapo Papers will be necessary to fully understand all of the intricacies, but we know that Lord Baltimore's fantasy was never realized.

When Cecil Calvert died, his vision of a utopia on the Nanti-coke River died with him. The Western Shore Alliance to Sup-press the Eastern Shore pilfered the Baltimore name and ap-plied it to a choice section of the real estate they had been holding in anticipation of the Industrial Revolution.

The Crapo Papers also inform us that a group of promi-nent Eastern Shore planters, men who had always been in sympathy with the plight of Delmarva's Native Americans, met at the site of Calvert's failed capital and decided to honor their friends, the Nanticoke Indians, by naming the commun-ity "Vienna" in honor of Vinnacokasimmon, the great emperor of the Nanticoke Nation.

The third vowel was added to the first two syllables of Vinnacokasimmon's name to deceive the Choptank Indians, who were living in Dorchester's Neck District and would, un-derstandably, have wanted a town named for their emperor as well. But as it turned out, the Choptanks were not so easily deceived. When their complaints of prejudice grew so loud and irrational as to constitute a public nuisance, they became known as the Red Neckers, but that's another story.

In naming Vienna, however, the planters, most of whom were illiterate, had failed to understand that in those days the letters V and U were transposed in the English language. A survey of documents from the period will quickly give proof to this. Vinnacokasimmon was really Unnacokasimmon, and anyone can verify this by checking the Maryland Historical Marker on Route 331 at the north end of Vienna.

The problem apparently went unnoticed for many years. Finally, the Crapo Papers reveal, when Thomas Holiday Hicks was elected to the Maryland legislature in 1829, he attempted to remedy the error by introducing legislation to change the name of Vienna to Unna. Hicks was born in East New Market, only a few miles from the Nanticoke River, and for several years lived in Vienna as a respected merchant.

We all know, of course, that Hicks went on to be elected governor of Maryland, in which capacity he served during the

Civil War. A friend of Abraham Lincoln, Hicks is credited with keeping Maryland in the Union by refusing to permit a meeting of the legislature at a time when it probably would have voted for secession. A rumor that Hicks failed to call the legislature into session because he was enjoying a particularly good run of bass fishing while on a trip to Deep Creek Lake in Western Maryland has finally been verified by the Crapo Papers.

In honor of Hicks memory, Eastern Shore delegates have unsuccessfully attempted to rectify the error of Vienna's designation over the years, most recently by attaching a rider to another of Delmarva's frequently repeated attempts at progress—a bill proposing that the Eastern Shore be permitted to secede from the rest of Maryland and form an independent nation.

Although these efforts have continued to fail (the Western Shore Alliance to Suppress the Eastern Shore having survived as a clandestine but highly effective part of the state's infrastructure), a senator from Oysterback hopes to quietly and unobtrusively tack the whole business onto next year's budget for the governor's mansion under the classification of plumbing improvements.

With certainty, had Cecil Calvert's original designs been realized, the history of Maryland—indeed, the history of the United States—would have evolved in a very different way.

Take the War of 1812 as one small example. We learn for the first time from our study of the Crapo Papers that the British admiral who was sent to capture Maryland's chief port relied entirely upon maps which he purchased from a spy, who turned out to be a cook for the Hoopers Island Militia. These charts, which were represented to the British as the latest word in intelligence, had been surreptitiously altered to show the original location of Baltimore; that is to say, the maps showed the city as being situated on the Nanticoke River adjacent to the Conectiv Power Company's generating plant. As a result, the British entered the Nanticoke River and sailed to Vienna, expecting to find Fort McHenry there. By the time their admiral discovered the ruse, he had spent most of his military allotment for the year.

To make matters worse, an itinerant preacher in a log canoe, whom the British commander summoned to deliver a sermon to his troops, informed them, instead, that if they ever did find Baltimore, they would have their butts thumped by the waiting defenders. The cleric also suggested that God might not deliver a kind judgment to men who would leave their wives and family behind to fend for themselves, while they sailed off across an ocean to pillage a bunch of relatives.

The facts are well known to history. When, after months of delay, the British forces finally arrived off the real Baltimore, their morale was low, they were short of supplies, and they were easily defeated by the American defenders.

Then we have the matter of our National Anthem, which everyone knows is an outgrowth of the British failure in Baltimore Harbor. Had the battle been fought at Vienna instead, it is unlikely that Francis Scott Key would have bothered to make the trip across the bay, it being a long and arduous journey in those days, and America would have no National Anthem today.

Like I said at the beginning: history is a funny thing; you just can't believe everything you read.

∞

When everything closed down in the big depression back in '29, Captain Henry and Mr. Nelson had some money in the Vienna bank, so they took up a shotgun and went down to see the banker where he lived. Captain Henry said, "Now you're gonna give us our money, ain't you?" That banker took 'em right to the bank.

∞

It Just Looks Old

"It's not old; it just looks old," the description accompanying the picture explained. And, indeed, the dimly lit figure of a primitive, black-faced angel, adorned in a weathered, white garment, had every appearance of belonging to a previous century.

"Gary White," another line beneath a close-up of the angel's face explained, "is a self-taught artist—a Visionary who is compulsed [sic] to create. Primitive, rustic, whimisical [sic], and having character and personality are words used by many who appreciate his art."

As I reclined in my swivel chair to dwell for a moment on the image, another vision bloomed from the back of my mind: that of an old, grizzled black man, perched amid a scattering of wood chips on the step of a sagging log hut, brow furrowed, penknife slowly peeling a fragrant wooden curl from a slab of cedar. Dateline: somewhere in southern Appalachia.

I was surfing through postings on eBay, the Internet's premier auction site. Bids for ownership of the black angel, in its last hour on the block, had risen to $86.75. The figure was described as being eleven inches tall by seven inches wide. It would, the text promised, be shipped anywhere in the world free of additional charge.

I would learn later that Gary White's art can be found in a wide variety of locations: shops, public buildings, private homes across the nation, and in several foreign countries. My surprise was to discover that he lived on Delmarva.

Like so many of us, White is a "come here," having been lured from his native Westminster, Maryland, by the slower pace of life and a real estate offer he couldn't turn down. Employing e-mail and telephone, I immediately began to negotiate for an interview, and we agreed on a time to meet.

At the appointed location I found a man in paint-spattered jeans and T-shirt, hard at work under a threatening sky filled with raucous, wheeling gulls. The blue tongue of a hissing acetylene torch licked up and down over the freshly painted form of another black angel, lightly singeing its finish to a weathered patina, adding years with each pass of the flame. At fifty inches in height, however, the lady was a bit more imposing than the ones I had seen on eBay.

"She's a beauty," I remarked, completing a full circle around the figure to observe it from all sides.

"It's going on eBay tonight," White said, cutting off the fuel to his torch.

"That's too bad; I was hoping I could buy it."

"Oh well," White quickly countered, "you're welcome to buy it."

"Your black angels must be pretty popular," I observed.

"Yeah, man," he responded, "the black angels are making me rich. They're just as ugly as the white ones, but people like them best. I just keep waiting for it to die down. But what gets me, (White's expression took on a puzzled look) the big ones aren't bringing any more than the little ones."

One of White's smaller angels sold at auction for $232 to a woman in Michigan. "I had to call her on the phone," the artist recalled. "I said, 'Listen, you know this angel is not old, don't you?' She said, 'I know, but my niece collects them.'

"People on the internet probably think I'm an old black man settin' on the porch," White continued with a half smile, "but I don't mean for them to think that. I had one guy came down from New York. He was going on vacation and stopped to see me. I said, 'You probably thought I was an old black man settin' on the porch, didn't you?' He says, 'Oh, no! no! I didn't

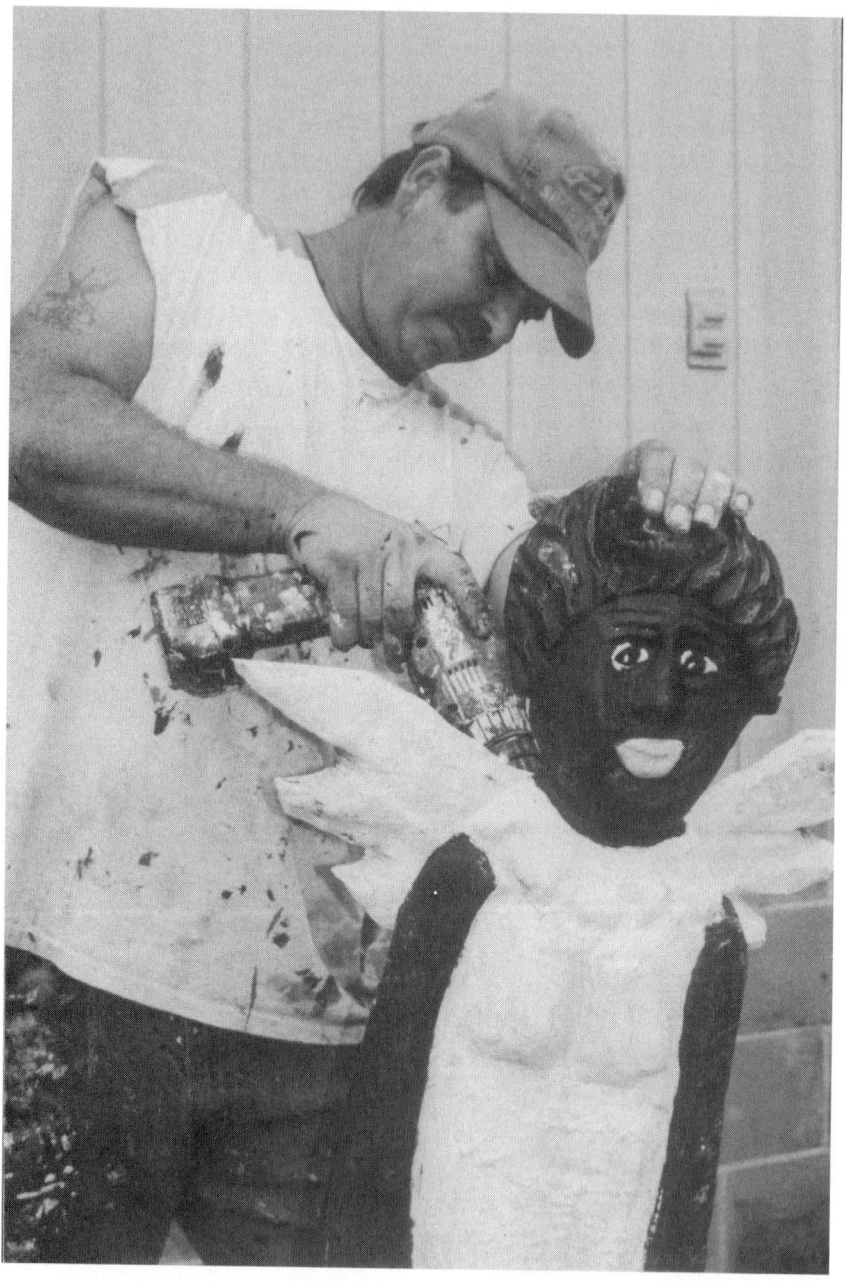

Gary White Attaching the Wings to a Black Angel

think that.' And his daughter says, 'Yeah you did!'"

I decided not to mention my own vision; instead, I asked, "How long have you been carving?"

"I guess maybe twenty years," White answered after a few seconds thought. "I was a carpenter for fifteen years. I like to fool around with wood. I've been doing this full time for the last three years."

While a carpenter, White spent a majority of his free time working flea markets, buying and selling a wide variety of merchandise. "Just flea market junk," he explained. "Then I started to throw in a few of my rough carvings, and I'd always sell them. I started selling more carvings than other things."

Today on eBay, White still sells an assortment of collectibles, but he no longer displays at flea markets. You may find him listing things like a Civil War bayonet, a cigarette lighter made in Occupied Japan, or a Ford backhoe. That last one got my attention. It turned out to be a fourteen-inch model.

"It's rough," White said, "but once in a while you'll get a piece that makes it worthwhile. I bought one item—it wasn't that old. I paid $13 for it, and I thought it was a little much, but it ended up going for $132 on eBay."

At the time we talked, White had been selling on eBay for about two months. "I know nothing about computers," he said, shaking his head. "All I know is how to turn it on. It took many, many hours to learn how to list things—many all-niters."

The wood White uses for most of his carving is very light in weight. "What kind of wood is this?" I asked, hefting the finished figure of a primitive fish.

"Paulownia," he answered.

"Paulownia!" I was dumbfounded. The paulownia or empress tree is native to China, but its large terminal clusters of fragrant violet flowers have made it popular as an ornamental, and it has become naturalized in the East as far north as New York City. You have probably heard or read about it. Tree rustlers are spiriting away specimens from farms and wood lots up and down the Delmarva Peninsula.

"What's the big deal?" you ask.

The big deal is that the wood of a fine, mature paulownia can bring up to $100 a board foot on the Japanese market; prime individual trees can be worth thousands of dollars.

White gets his logs from the Westminster area. "It's paulownia," he says, "but it's no good to anybody. It's not the stuff the Japanese are interested in."

White sometimes substitutes sassafras and occasionally carves in pine. He is allergic to cedar. "I've used it," he said, "but I can hardly breathe when I do."

For a while White sold his work from a shop in Chincoteague, Virginia, but he now markets exclusively on the internet and to retail outlets. "I mostly supply stores in Baltimore and Ellicott City. I sell a lot to the American Visionary Arts Museum."

Some of his carvings have gone to Russia, England, and Japan, and he used to have an outlet in California, the Zoo Gallery on Santa Monica Boulevard.

"How did this all start?" I wanted to know.

"Just playing around with the chain-saw," White replied casually. He has done chain-saw carving but is quick to admit, "I'm not a chain-saw artist, but that's what I use to start a piece."

White first cuts slabs of wood from a section of tree trunk with his chain-saw. For rough shaping he utilizes an angle grinder mounted with a small saw chain, which he calls a "lancelot." A dado or straight-cut router bit mounted on a second power tool is next employed, and for final shaping, a wood rasp. The result is a rustic, primitive carving with a lot of country appeal.

White paints the finished object, then singes it with an acetylene torch. "I burn it to get an antique effect," he said. After the first application of flame, he wire brushes the figure, then burns it and brushes it a second time. "It gives them that older look. I always tell people that my things are painted to make them look old, but they're not old."

White uses a variety of paint. "It's whatever I have," he explained. "If I run out of black, the next one's going to be a white angel. That's just the way it is." And then he added, "I'm color blind."

"So that's why her lips are green," I quipped, pointing to the figure in front of us.

"Are they green?" he asked with mild concern. "Do you want her lips red?"

"I'm teasing you."

"Oh, OK. I have made green people, but they looked flesh-colored to me. You know those books the doctors have you look at to pick the number out. I can't see one of them."

White makes fish, turtles, foxes, deer, bears, just about every kind of wildlife there is. "I do a lot of alligators; they're pretty popular. I did a couple crabs. I had one giant crab I stuck on the roof, and a guy drove by and wanted to buy it. Things don't last long.

"If I make a mistake, I don't throw it away. I just fix it or make it into something else. I've had wooden Indians that I've turned into bears and bears I've turned into Indians. I might cut a head off, then carve another one and nail it on."

"What sells best," I asked, "aside from the black angels?"

"The stores that I deal with in Baltimore and Elliott City want the animals, but on eBay they love the people." In addition to angels, White carves santas (many of them black), Civil War soldiers and their wives, Indians, nuns, etc.

Until recently, dealers were gobbling up everything White could produce at wholesale prices. On eBay he is finally getting the payment he deserves. "eBay," he said, "is a whole new audience, and you get a good idea of what your stuff is really worth. I've been guessing for fifteen years."

I asked how many individual objects he completes in a year.

"Oh, I don't know—a lot. I usually make four or five pieces every day." White figures he has fashioned and sold over three thousand items.

In addition to wood, White uses other material in his sculptures. Parts are frequently metal, like the fins on a fish, and on one nun carving he filled a knothole with automobile body putty, and that became the face.

In the morning, before he begins to work, White will often check a few dumpsters.

"A lot of times I find junk I can use: wood, metal, broken stuff—just about anything. If it looks like I can make something out of it, I take it. I found an old tool box tray. One part of the tray was broken but the other part had a handle. I cut an angel out of it, and the angel hangs on the handle.

"I found a round piece of barrel top that somebody used for target practice—shot bullet holes through it—so I picked it up and threw it in the back of the truck. I cut a rooster out of it, put a chain on it, and painted it. It looked good. I put it on eBay and said, 'This is a rooster that used to hang out by the house, and some redneck came by and shot it one night.' I got an e-mail saying, 'A redneck wouldn't waste his time on that bird.'"

"Most people would throw this piece in the fireplace," I remarked, pointing to a section of tree trunk which decay had hollowed over the years and from which many slabs had been removed by White's chain saw. "What are *you* going to do with it?"

"That has just about had it," he conceded. Then, looking at it closely, as though for the first time, he said, "Well, I think I can make an umbrella stand out of that."

White also constructs what he terms "twig furniture," utilitarian pieces fashioned from natural, rough sections of tree limbs.

"Usually when I make a twig chair," he explained, picking up a long curving piece of driftwood, "I make the back out of something like this."

Another weathered limb on the stockpile attracted his attention. "There's a lady wants a swan, so I'll probably do a swan out of that." Then he quickly added, "I don't do decoys.

I'm just too primitive, I guess."

"So is this your future?" I asked.

"Oh yeah, I'll never work for anybody again. This is it!"

I was interested in knowing how White's work has evolved, what changes he has made over the years.

"I've done a little bit of everything," he offered. "When I get tired of making something—when it's not fun anymore—I just start making something else. If I get an order for twelve of one thing, that takes the fun right out of it; that makes it work."

White is forty-two, has been married for twenty-four years, and has two children. His son is presently assigned to a naval base in Japan. White, himself, served a hitch in the Navy back in the seventies.

After negotiating a price, we loaded the still-damp angel into the back of my van. As I pulled out onto the road to leave, I called to White across the lot, "I think you should go check the dumpster now."

"I might do that," he grinned back at me.

∞

Old John lived down there on the neck with his son, Tommy, and he had a great old black bull he would rent out to anybody had a cow they wanted took care of. One day John and Tommy was off huntin', and this fella from up 'round Car'line come down there, and he wanted to see John. Weren't nobody 'round but the hired man, and he told the fella that John and his boy had went off huntin'.

"Well," the fella says, "his son has my daughter in a family way, and I come to settle with 'em."

"Well, I can't help you none there," the hired man says. "John gits five dollars for the bull, but I don't know what he charges for Tommy."

∞

The Lady on the Road

Life is energy, and scientists inform us that energy can neither be created nor destroyed—it can only change form.

Some people believe that a ghost consists of the energy which was once part of a human being and that, in spite of having lost the vehicle of a body, it continues to possess and exhibit all the mental attributes of a living person.

We hear about a multitude of ghost sightings, some of which are deliberately fabricated, while others have blossomed in the minds of the superstitious or were generated by a failure to understand what was being observed. But we also have those which cannot so easily be explained away.

A woman told me once, "People are always wondering—was that something supernatural that went bump in the night, but if you are ever fortunate enough to encounter a ghost or have one attempt to communicate with you, there will be no question about what you are seeing."

American folklore is replete with legends of ghosts who frequent roadsides. Most are female, and generally they are young and attractive. Some are hitchhikers; others seem simply to be waiting or wandering.

A stretch of highway near Little Rock, Arkansas, boasts a number of vanishing hitchhiker stories. One driver picked up a young woman who requested a ride home, only to have her disappear at the given address. Bewildered, the good Samaritan knocked on the cottage door. The elderly man who answered nodded when told the story. "My daughter was killed on this day a long time ago," he said, "and each year she finds someone like you to bring her home."

In a similar story, a man agreed to transport a girl to a residence in Woodson. When they arrived, she asked the driver to please knock on the door before she got out. A woman responded, and the man informed her that he had brought her daughter home. Horrified, the woman said that her daughter had died one year ago on that very night. They rushed to the man's car. Except for a blue coat left on the front seat, the vehicle was empty. "My God," the woman gasped, "it's her coat!"

Another tale includes a bridge near Batesville, where a lone motorist picked up a bruised and battered hitchhiker one night in 1973. The girl claimed to have been in an accident and asked for a ride home. When the man attempted to assist her to the door, she vanished. A gentleman who responded to the driver's excited knocks claimed that his daughter had died a month earlier in an accident at the bridge near Batesville. For more than a quarter of a century, this same girl has been flagging down unsuspecting travelers and requesting a ride home.

Similarly, in Greensboro, North Carolina, numerous reports have been filed of a young woman who stands next to the US 70 underpass. She wears a white evening gown and waves frantically for drivers to stop and pick her up. The hapless traveler who consents is introduced to "Lydia," who asks to be driven to an address in High Point. She has spent the evening at a dance in Raleigh, she claims, and is anxious to get home. As the vehicle approaches the designated house, the girl vanishes. She is simply there one minute and gone the next. If the driver inquires at the residence, he is told that Lydia died while coming home from a dance in Raleigh, the victim of a car crash at the US 70 underpass.

In a remote area of Kentucky, a few miles north of the Tennessee border, two young men were driving along Meshack Road on their way to a barn dance when they came upon an attractive young woman. She accepted their invitation to accompany them and enjoyed dancing with both boys during the evening. Afterward, she agreed to let them drive her home. By the time they arrived, it had begun to rain. One of the boys offered the girl his coat, saying he would pick it up the next day. But when he returned and inquired for the girl, the woman of the house informed him that her only daughter had died sometime before in an accident on Meshack Road. The boy asked where the girl was buried, and when he went to the churchyard, he found his coat beside her grave.

Dances are frequently part of the theme with roadside ghosts. Resurrection Mary, a blonde-haired, blue-eyed beauty who has been seen since the late 1930s, is Chicago's most famous ghost. According to legend, Mary attended a dance at the O'Henry Ballroom, now called Willowbrook. She got into an argument with her boyfriend and decided to hitchhike home. Somewhere on Archer Avenue between the Willowbrook and the main gates of Resurrection Cemetery, she was struck and killed by a hit-and-run driver.

The first account of Mary's ghost came from Jerry Palus, a south-side man who recently died. He is reported to have picked up a girl on Archer Avenue and danced with her the entire evening. Later, she requested a ride home and directed Jerry past Resurrection Cemetery. As they approached the graveyard, the girl told him to pull over. She got out and ran toward the main gates, vanishing before she reached them.

One of the most gripping disclosures of an encounter with Mary was reported in a newspaper article written by Bill Geist and published in the Suburban Tribune on January 31, 1979. Ralph, a cab driver, tells his story:

> It was Thursday night—would have been two weeks ago—and I was basically lost. I'd dropped this big spender way the hell down in Palos Heights or Hills or someplace like that and was trying to make my way back to the tollway. I'd just turned onto Archer, down there where it's still a lonely road, especially at midnight.
>
> And there she was. She was standing there with no coat on, by the entrance to this little shopping center. No coat! and

it was one of those real cold ones, too.

She didn't put out her thumb or nothing like that. She just looked at my cab. Of course I stopped. I figured maybe she had car trouble or something.

She hopped right in the front seat. She had on this fancy kind of white dress, like she'd just been to a wedding or something, and those kind of disco-type shoes with straps and that.

She was a looker. A blond. I didn't have ideas or like that; she was young enough to be my daughter—twenty-one tops.

I asked her where she was going, and she said she had to get home. I asked her what was wrong, if she'd had car trouble or what, but she really didn't answer me. She was fuzzy, like maybe she'd had a couple of drinks or something or was just tired. I don't know.

Oh, the only thing she did say really was, "The snow came early this year," or, "The snows came early," or like that. Other than that she just nodded when I asked if we were supposed to keep going up Archer. She was just looking out the window at the snow and the trees and that. Her mind was a million miles away, like maybe she smoked something, or who knows?

A couple miles up Archer, she jumped with a start like a horse and said, "Here! Here!" I hit the brakes.

I looked around and didn't see no kind of house. "Where?" I said. And then she sticks out her arm and points across the road to my left and says, "There!"

And that's when it happened.

I looked to my left, like this, and when I turned, she was gone. Vanished!

And the car door never opened. May the good Lord strike me dead, it never opened.

Some legends predate the age of motorized vehicles.

She was a frail woman, they say, dressed in white and with a look of great sadness in her eyes. Her fiancé had struck it rich in the gold fields in the 1850s and had sent for her to join him in California to be married. On the journey west she fell ill and perished in the Vallecito Stagecoach Station. She was buried in an unmarked grave a few hundred yards into the desert. Campers and hikers still occasionally report a lady in white, restlessly pacing the worn earth where the adobe station once stood, waiting for the stage to Sacramento.

Years ago, when Delmarva roads were darker and rutted by the narrow wheels of wagons and horse carts, another lady in white is said to have been frequently observed in the vicinity of Henry's Crossroads in Dorchester County. She is reported to have displayed little interest in travelers and sometimes ascended a large pine tree before disappearing into a fog.

During a book signing at Blackwater National Wildlife Refuge, a gentleman stopped at my table and inquired about the contents of the volumes stacked in front of me. He was Paul Bellezza. I explained that I collected tales of history and folklore on Delmarva.

"Let me tell you some folklore," he quickly offered. "We live in Fishing Creek, and this road—335 past Meekins Neck—is haunted."

Bellezza's pretty daughter, Danielle, joined us in time to hear her dad's last sentence and pronounced with a flair: "The lady in black!"

Bellezza continued: "I went to town this day and was coming back after eleven at night. It was September 19th. I was driving down the road just past Meekins Neck Road, where the church is, and I saw something about a third of a mile in front of me. I saw these buttons glowing, but I didn't know they were buttons then. I got closer and saw it was a woman dressed in a black, three-quarter-length dress with long sleeves, and she had black, pointy shoes that were laced. The dress material was like cotton; the light didn't reflect from it the way it does from polyester. I slowed down and thought, 'What's she doing here?' I thought maybe she broke down. I put my bright lights on as I came up to her and started rolling down the window. She was coming toward me on the opposite side of the road. She had blonde-reddish hair in a bob, and she was beautiful—I mean she was stunning and very well kept. She put her hand up to block the bright lights, and I saw she was wearing long, black gloves. All of a sudden I thought, 'Oh, oh, something's wrong here,' and I took off. When I looked around, she was gone—completely gone.

"I took off and went home. When I pulled in my driveway, I sat there to get my breath a minute, and a car went by. They were the people from three doors down.

"My wife was in bed. I said, 'Mary, you've got to come with me.' I told her the story, but she wouldn't get up.

"So I went over and talked to my neighbors. I said, 'You just came down the road about three minutes after me. Did you see a woman walking the road?'

"They said, 'We didn't see anything.'"

Bellezza's wife had joined us while he was telling the story and volunteered, "He was white as a ghost; he was really scared. And as soon as he told me, the hair on the back of my neck stood straight up. He said, 'I know you won't believe it.' I said, 'Well, I do believe you.' You can tell when somebody is really distressed just from the way they are acting."

"We would have gone," Danielle interrupted, "but Mommy had just put me to sleep."

"I was a mess," admitted Bellezza, and then added, "Later I was talking to a girl whose family has lived down here for a hundred and fifty or two hundred years. She says that other people have seen a woman—the ghost of a woman—who walks that road at night."

As might be expected, there are some who view the lady on the road with skepticism. I asked a man whose family ties extend three centuries back through south Dorchester history for his opinion.

"I've lived at Meekins Neck," he said, "but I've never heard of it." Then he paused for a moment and offered, "Well, I did know of some ladies that walked the road, but you wouldn't want to write a story about it?"

∞

"Of Course You Can't Print It"

Every now and then I am told a story which is accompanied by a statement like: "Of course you can't print it." Sometimes I agree, and other times. . . well, you decide.

Now here's a good one for you; of course you can't print it. My grandfather was a great one for British Oil. I mean he believed in it. I've taken a many a bit of it. There was an old guy who used to come in town with an old horse and an old derbin—I can see him now. His name was George. Anyhow, this boy out where George lived had caught himself a dose of the crabs, and he asked Mr. George if he knew of anything for 'em. He said, "No, but you go to town. . . ," and he told him how to find Grandfather. "You ask him," George told the boy, "and I'll guarantee he can tell you what to do to get rid of 'em."

So the boy come down, and Grandfather said, "Have you got any British Oil?"

"No," he said. He'd never heard of it.

Grandfather said, "Well, you go down to the drugstore here and ask Dubie."

Well, anyhow, he got the British Oil—it was an over-the-shelf thing—and he went home. Grandfather had told him to just wash his whole bottom end in the stuff.

About two weeks later, old man George come down there, and he said to Grandfather, "What in this world did you tell that boy to do?" He said, "Whatever it was, he's been goin' a-round holdin' onto his balls ever since."

∞

You never knew Mary-Lou, now did you? She was—let me see now, how am I gonna tell it? Mary-Lou had a reputa-tion, let's say, for bein' just a little free with her favors, and it happened one time she come near to closin' old Eddie up over it. She used to come down to the store there when the boys would hang out. It got so the other womenfolk, they did-n't want their men a-comin' down there.

So one day Eddie, he told her, "Look here now, Mary-Lou, it makes me a lot of trouble, you comin' in and hangin' out. I'm losin' business, and I don't want you around no more."

Well, that set a match right to Mary-Lou's tinder, and she went home in a stew. That evenin', when the boys was packed right full in there, settin' 'round drinkin' sodas and tellin' tales, Mary-Lou come on back down. She looked that bunch over hard, then she stood there with her hands on her hips, and she said, "I'm pregnant! and the next time I come in here, if the father's around, I'm a-gonna tell his name." And she went on back home.

Well, everybody all of a sudden remembered somethin' they had to do, and after that the boys were as scarce around Ed-die's as hen's teeth, least way they had somebody on lookout, you know, should Mary-Lou be a-comin' down the road.

Course it turned out she weren't pregnant at all, but things never was the same around Eddie's after that.

∞

A Man of Character

Nestled among aging cedars on a quiet hill overlooking Federalsburg, Maryland, a small gravestone bears the inscription:

ROBERT W MESSENGER
CPL 5 MD INF
SP AM WAR
FEB 23 1870   MAY 8 1948

Although once a giant among area businessmen, the man who lies beneath this monument has been all but forgotten.

I like to tell people that Robert Messenger and Margaret Mitchell have something in common—they each wrote a single novel. Everyone knows about *Gone With The Wind,* but how many have even heard of *Patty Cannon Administers Justice?*

The novel, self published by Messenger in 1926, addresses several days in the life of Delmarva's most notorious woman criminal while blatantly ignoring historical fact. Fewer than a thousand copies of the small, brown volume were manufactured by J. W. Stowell Printing Company in Federalsburg.

Judge Marvin Smith's father was a Linotype operator for Stowell and set the type for Messenger's book. "My father always vowed and declared," said Judge Smith, "that if the author had been anyone other than Bob Messenger, that book would have sold."

Literary critics have not been as kind, but in spite of poor

Robert W. Messenger in 1898

reviews and the author's own comment that it is "a story without much real merit," the novel was reprinted in 1960 by Tidewater Publishers.

It is not always an easy task to separate the life of Robert William from that of his older brother, Henry Burdette Messenger. In many ventures they were partners. Robert is usually identified by the initials R. W., while Henry preferred to be called H. B. or Burdette.

"Late in the 1630s," Donald Messenger, H. B.'s grandson, informed me, "another pair of Messenger brothers, Andrew and Henry, emigrated from Yorkshire, England." That Henry, whose given name has been passed from generation to generation, had thirteen children, one of whom migrated to western Massachusetts and settled near the small town of Peru. It was there in the Berkshire Hills, generations later, where R. W. and H. B. were born. Their father's name was Henry A.

About 1880, after contracting tuberculosis, Henry A. sought a warmer climate and moved his family to Delmarva, to the Northwest Branch of the Nanticoke River. It was here that his sons would pursue their fortune, an odyssey resulting first in enormous success, then crushing failure.

No physical evidence remains of the Messenger enterprises which once sprawled along the Maryland and Delaware Railroad tracks and the shores of Marshyhope Creek in Federalsburg. They began about 1887 with a cannery to process tomatoes from surrounding farms. Altogether, I have discovered ten canneries owned or partly owned by the Messengers—two others in Federalsburg, one each in Farmington and Oak Grove, Delaware, and four in Dorchester County, Maryland. Among family photographs is one of a plant labeled "Keller, Virginia," but I have not been able to verify its ownership.

When the Spanish-American War erupted in 1898, Robert enlisted in Company E of the 5th Maryland Volunteers. The only information the family has of his service during the three-month war is written on the back of a Company E photograph taken at Tampa, Florida, in July, 1898. After identifying himself and others in the picture, Messenger wrote:

> About 20 comrades were in West Tampa Hospital. We were moved to Huntsville, Ala. to get us away from typhoid which usually followed dengue fever. Nearly all of us had dengue fever (Fla. malaria) and nearly half of 106 men in [the] company had typhoid. I was one of 6 out of 106 who was never on sick report, but I had dengue fever, which got me down to 129 pounds. I kept our doctor from finding out I had the malaria although it took 28 pounds off me in three days and burned me out, because so many of our boys who were sent to the West Tampa Hospital with dengue fever contracted typhoid fever in the hospital.

Two hundred years before the Messengers arrived on the Marshyhope, a dam had been constructed and a grist mill erected near the present site of Federalsburg. By the late nineteenth century, Idewild Mill had become the best equipped water-powered facility on the peninsula south of Wilmington, Delaware. During dry seasons, however, water power often failed, causing considerable inconvenience to the town and surrounding countryside.

In 1900, to alleviate these periodic hardships, the Messengers built the powerful, steam-operated Eagle Mill at the lower end of town, on its own side track and with wharves along the river front. Large quantities of grain were imported, and the mill's products were distributed by Messenger boats and by rail. In 1904 it was heralded as the best equipped mill on Delmarva.

Across the railroad tracks from Eagle Mill stood a can factory owned by the Messenger brothers and two partners. A period advertisement identifies the Federal Can Company as "makers of fine locked steam cans" with the "largest capacity of any can plant on the peninsula."

R. W. took a special interest in can manufacturing and invented a process for cutting can ends. His granddaughters remember their father and aunt being involved in litigation concerning patent infringement, but the details have been forgotten. "He was always so ethical," granddaughter Lynn Messenger said. "He let people run over him."

Around the turn of the century the Messengers also had interests in a mill where wood was split into kindling and shipped loose in railroad cars or barges to wholesalers in cities, and they may have owned a box factory.

In Ellenor Merriken's *Herring Hill*, R. W. and H. B. are credited with building the first shell road in Federalsburg. They also engaged in road construction throughout Caroline and Dorchester Counties in partnership with Tom Holt.

Around 1915, Robert built a home on Central Avenue in Federalsburg, a few blocks from the river and the site of a thriving Messenger business center. The five-bedroom mansion was constructed of a distinctive yellow brick with a terra cotta roof. "R. W. told me after World War II," Judge Smith said, "that he built the house for $15,000."

There are differences of opinion as to what caused Robert's financial decline and the eventual loss of his home and businesses. Some say it was a post WW I collapse in the tomato market; others blame the depression. I found the answer in copies of two letters, which granddaughter Robin Jameson owns. The letters were written when Messenger enrolled his son in Mercersburg Academy in 1924.

One is addressed to the Academy and signed by Philetus Jefferson, head cashier at the Federalsburg First National Bank [now Atlantic Bank]:

> In replying to your letter of inquiry regarding William Ashley Messenger, let me assure you there is not a more honest and deserving young boy in our town. His home influences have been excellent and his father's means are at present limited because of the rascality of others—especially the Eastern Shore Brokage Company—a defunct canned goods brokage firm (composed of leading financiers of this locality) who debased their contract with Mr. Messenger . . . after the close of the war and have petitioned for bankruptcy to cause

him and others severe financial losses.

The second document was written to the Academy by R. W. and includes the following statement:

> Starting with nothing I built myself gradually up to being worth $30,000 to $40,000 when war was declared in 19-17. I was a veteran of the Spanish-American War myself, my great grandfather was a captain in the Revolutionary War, and I took my duties seriously enough (being overage myself) to refuse to profiteer one dollar during 1917 and 1918. Most canners did profiteer unmercifully and I became rather a "pariah" because I did not "pack with my fellows." Naturally, as generally happens, deflation hit me harder than it did the ones who profiteered, in addition to which my brother and a partner were both put absolutely down and out and lost me large sums of money. For the past three years I have been staving off bankruptcy only by strenuous effort, but think matters are on the upturn for good now.

R. W. was wrong!

"Our aunt always said that he signed promissory notes for seven people," granddaughter Lynn told me. "All of them had their notes called in, and Grandfather lost his money and his home. None of them ever paid him back."

R. W. moved to Pocomoke City after his financial world collapsed; no one in the family knows where or for whom he worked. His last days were spent in Salisbury.

Although Messenger produced only a single book in his lifetime, he was a prolific writer of letters, many of which were published in Maryland newspapers. His outspoken criticism of Franklin Roosevelt, according to his granddaughters, brought him under investigation by that administration. Following is an excerpt from one of Messenger's early World War II missives:

> To The Editor of The Sun—Sir:
> For over forty years the Japanese desired a war with us. For over forty years they felt they would lose such a war if

they started it. Then, as the New Deal developed into the Raw Deal, they saw their chance and grasped it. They prepared thoroughly for it, they launched it and, until this country rids itself of Raw Deal influences, they have won it.

The time has come to amend our earnest desire to "get behind Roosevelt." We must "get ahead of Roosevelt," if we want to win the war before we have frittered away our resources to the point of national bankruptcy.

We should have realized long ago that we must rescind the most detestable class legislation this country has ever known, and thus bring in a Square Deal to replace the Raw Deal. Until we do these things our great resources cannot be employed. The splendid spirit of our young men will only bring about their sacrifice instead of a glorious victory over evil forces.

R. W. MESSENGER—Salisbury, Md.

I have met only a few people who knew Messenger personally. Judge Smith told me, "When I first remember him, he was riding his bicycle and had an office in the First National Bank Building. He was a baseball player and played till an older age than most did—a better than average player. He and his brother H. B. were both great boat men."

The Messenger brothers were also avid cyclists. In *Those Cambridge Cracks*, a chronology of the Cambridge Cycle Club by Claude Gootee, R. W. is listed on the February 5, 1898 membership roster, and H. B. won a racing trophy which his grandson Donald still displays.

Miriam Thomas was nine when her grandfather passed away. She remembers him meeting her after school with licorice treats. "I have absolutely wonderful memories of him," she told me. "He was very refined, very dignified, very caring, very loving, very giving. He was a man of high moral character."

One of the mysteries which remains about R. W. Messenger is why, at the age of fifty-six, in dire financial straits, he chose to write and self-publish the novel about Patty Cannon. One claim is that the book was an attempt to "soften Patty's

R. W. Messenger in Later Years

image as projected in *The Entailed Hat*."

And why would Messenger want to do that?

"To help out the Cannons in Bridgeville, who were cousins of Patty's husband," I was told.

Indeed, the Bridgeville Cannons, who were direct descendants of Delaware Governor William Cannon and managed one of the leading canneries in the region, were very distantly related to Jesse Cannon, but the hypothesis that Messenger wrote the book for that reason is absurd.

R. W. Messenger died in Fort Howard Hospital in 1948 at the age of seventy-eight. He was survived by his wife, a son, a daughter, and two granddaughters. A third granddaughter would be born later.

Postscript

In spite of at least ten Messenger canneries, I have never come across a Messenger check or token as they are commonly called. For many years it was the custom to account for a worker's production by issuing metal tokens. These were later exchanged for spendable currency. Cannery checks have become a much-sought-after collectable in recent years.

R. Lee Burton is the author of a wonderfully informative little book, *Canneries of the Eastern Shore*. Although it illustrates hundreds of tokens, none are Messengers.

I called Lee.

"I went to see Mrs. Messenger [H. B.'s daughter-in-law, Esther] when she was still living," Burton told me, "and asked her about tokens. She said they used aluminum tokens, but she didn't have any. I've never found one, and I'll tell you, I've really looked."

∞

A Messenger Cannery above—Eagle Mills below: Circa 1904

Two Pieces of Clothes

Her name was Beulah, and when we first talked, she told me she was ninety-five years old. Although traditional documents used to verify birth dates apparently do not exist for Beulah, what we know with certainty is that the clock of the twentieth century ticked off few days without her presence to witness them.

When I asked Beulah how many children she had brought into this world and how many lived to reach maturity, she struggled for an answer. It was clear there were many—more than sixteen. I did not press her to remember. She told me that seven were living.

The first child of a large family, Beulah was born in April. Half a dozen deliveries later, one of her siblings chose a raw, snowy, midwinter dawn to draw her first breath. Beulah remembered this about the birth of her sister:

"My mother was give a birth. She grannied [delivered] her ownself an' got right back in the bed. [She] take some cotton, made a little thing, an' put the belly ban' on. An' after she give the birth, she wrap the baby up. We didn't have no fire, an' it was cold an' snowy. Momma went out the house in a little thicket place an' cut a rotten tree down an' got the inside out—the lighter, we used to call it. You know, that's what they lit on. It kept just like it had oil in it. [The day was] cold as ice, an' Momma [had] no shoes on an' no stockin's, an' she split the wood.

"An' when she come back in the house with it in her arm,

she said, 'If I die, I just die, an' if I live, I live—that's all. I gonna put it in God's hands.'

"She come back with the pieces of wood for she split up—real thin. She didn't have no coal oil to start that fire with, just had two matches—two matches that you strike. An' she got some straw. You know we slept then on a straw bed. Momma tore her mattress open an' got some straw out the bed an' put it in the stove. An' she lay those splinter of wood on top each other. She had one piece of paper, an' she struck that one match. An' that match catched that paper an' straw an' caught the stove up.

"We children was standin' 'round the stove just tremblin' cold. She [got] hot, that stove. Them old tin heaters, you know, they turn red; they turn real red when they get hot. We children go all up around the stove—cold as we could be—an' Momma got back in the bed with the baby. An' after [the] house got hot, she taken a sheet an' made the baby a little robe [to] put on, an' she said, 'Get me some water, children, so I [can] bath my baby.' An' that child [is] livin' today. I just can't 'member how old I was then—I was big enough to wash dishes.

"It snowed so [much that] my father—he [had] gone to Pocomoke, an' he couldn't get home. He work in the steam mill. He went days an' come back nights, but the snow [was] too heavy for him [to] come back home. He didn't know she gonna take sick, you know; couldn't get no granny woman or nothin' like that."

In the early part of the century, especially in rural areas, many children died from diseases. Diphtheria, influenza, and other afflictions were often the agents of deadly epidemics. Doctors were scarce, poorly equipped, and offered little in the way of help, and many people could not afford them.

"My sisters had spine geetis [spinal meningitis]," Beulah remembered. "The doctor told my mother, 'Don't let none of the children go around them but one—the oldest one.' I was the oldest one, an' they quarantine me in with 'em. Nobody could come out [of] the kitchen in[to] the front room where they was layin'. Two sisters had it in one room.

"An' when they fed me, they pushed it through the middle door so none the rest [of the] children wouldn't get hold of it, an' I couldn't get with the rest [of the] children."

One of the sisters became very ill.

"Momma said, 'They don't allow me in there to see my children, so I went to sleep an' dreamed 'bout somethin' I take an' bath my child in.' She said, 'If God [will] help me today, I'm goin' in the room where my child is. Now I'm goin' down [to] the drugstore.' An' she went in town to the drugstore an' didn't have a penny, an' she told her troubles. An' the drugstore man let her have it. She come home, put a little foot tub with water an' pour her stuff in that, an' she bath that child all over.

"[The] next two days my sister didn't know nothin'. First thing she [said was]: 'Momma! Momma!'

"Momma said, 'Oh, my Lord, my child [is] talkin'.'

"But she couldn't talk—just laid there hollerin'. It just bend her right on back. She was layin' on her haid, on her back, an' you could get a pillow under her back. It turned her another different shape.

"She laid like that for a long time, an' then she died. One of 'em died, an' the other live. An' I shroud her my ownself; give her bath; comb her hair; put her clothes on; put [a] sheet over her.

"An' [it] was the biggest snow you ever seen [in] your life, an' she had to lay in there near 'bout two weeks, an' I had to stay in there with her. I slept right in there with her. They couldn't take her nowhere at all. They didn't embalm people in them days—but one thing, it wasn't hot."

I asked Beulah one day about school. Where did she go to school? Was it fun?

"I didn't get to school," she told me. "My parents sent me, but the children mettled me so bad, so I ducked school. That's one thing I shouldn't o' did, but them children used to wrap up brickbats an' chunk 'em at me. I was scared of the children; I was really scared of 'em. So I ain't got a whole lot o' learnin' now. I didn't go a year in the first grade."

Beulah's father left the family when she was still very young.

"Poppa an' Momma didn't get along too good," Beulah told me matter-of-factly, "an' he jumped up an' left." Almost as an afterthought she added, "Poppa liked extra women. People didn't get divorced in them days," she explained. "They just left each other. The women took the children, an' they growed 'em up. The men got married again, but the women didn't. The men married three or four different women.

"We come up hard. Sometime we get a meal, an' sometime we don't get a meal all day long an' all night.

"Comin' up, I didn't have no shoes to put on my feet, no stockin's to put on my legs. Run through the woods; get briers in my feet. Sit down somewhere an' pull the briers out. In the wintertime snow come up to our knees—barefoot. But it didn't hurt me. I didn't have no shoes an' no stockin' till I was thirteen year old. But you know, we fared better then than we do now; we didn't hardly get a cold. When I commenced growin' up, my mother went an' got me shoes an' stockin's. I thought I was dressed up then.

"I got one [clean] dress a month an' one slip a month. We didn't have but two pieces of clothes to put on, just a slip an' a dress—no coat. Momma used to sit down an' make the dresses.

"Hardly anybody had any money. Momma used to go out in the woods an' get merkle bark. She cut the tree down an' get the root. After she cut aroun' that tree, Momma [would] pull the root out'n the ground an' carry 'em up to the house. She would wash it off good an' let it dry good. Then she'd take a hammer an' break that crust off'n it, you know, get the peelin' off the root. She carry it to the store, an' they buy it from her like that. That's how she got money for our little dresses.

"After Poppa left, these white people mostly raised me. Momma had so many children, so Mr. Tom looked at me an' [he said], 'I like that little girl; can't I have her?'

"Momma said, 'Yes, you can get her, but you let her come home every week to see me an' go back.' I was nine, ten years old, an' that's what I did.

"I slept on the floor, an' they slept on the bed—him an' his wife—an' I slept right in their room. He spread me quilts on the floor—old pillow against my haid. I didn't know no better; I felt just like I was in the bed. He'd whip me as good as he whip his children. [If] I did somethin' wrong [or] said somethin' wrong, he'd get a switch an' put it on me."

Beulah's life was long and full, replete with hardships that I never saw etched on her face. Instead, her features caught and held the moments of joy, which also were many in number, and for which Beulah daily offered her thanks. When she died in 1999, her obituary said she was one hundred and three years old.

∞

Some time ago, on a sparkling spring day on the Lloyd estate in Talbot County, Elizabeth Lloyd Shiller, who was then age ninety-seven, said to her cook, "Mary, I want to give a large luncheon. Use all the best linen and china. Have the silver polished to a high gleam. Use only the finest wines and champaign, and I want a delicious menu."

Astonished, Mary replied, "Of course, Miss Elizabeth, but who are you going to have as guests."

With a charming smile, Elizabeth replied, "All my friends in the graveyard."

Mary drew a deep breath. "Miss Elizabeth," she said, "I'll cook for 'em, but I ain't waitin' on 'em."

∞

It Was The Law

Volumes have been written about antiquated laws which, in retrospect, often amuse or shock us. Maryland certainly has had its share.

Colonial planters and watermen were apparently a profane lot indeed. Inappropriate language was used to such an extent that proprietary officials passed an ordinance which dictated a fine of ten pounds of tobacco for anyone found guilty of cursing or swearing. If an individual developed his talents to the degree where he became known as a "common swearer," punishment could be administered in any way the court saw fit.

Captain Thomas Bradnox, Justice of the Peace in Kent County, was one who achieved the status of "common swearer." After uttering at least a hundred oaths, which included calling one man a "loggerhead, puppy, and fool," Bradnox was fined three hundred pounds of tobacco.

When Sheriff James Vetch approached Michael Baisey, asking to borrow his grindstone, Baisey was quoted as replying, "God's blood, I will be the death of that man that shall fetch it away." For swearing at the sheriff, Baisey paid ten pounds in tobacco and had to give "sureties for good future behavior."

In an argument with Thomas Ringgold over a steer, Gregory Murell also swore "by God's blood," and in a dispute with William Elliott was said to have uttered "a great oath." After additional allegations that he swore "many outrageous, desperate, and bitter oaths," the county commissioners decided that Murell was a "common swearer" and fined him three hundred pounds of tobacco.

Apparently swearing was not the exclusive province of males. John Salter discovered that it paid to keep one's wife subdued when Kent County officials ordered him to pay ten pounds of tobacco for each of two oaths sworn by Mrs. Salter.

Under the Roman Catholic proprietors of early Maryland, the Sabbath was taken very seriously. By the terms of the Toleration Act of 1649, fines were imposed for anyone who profaned the Lord's Day by swearing, drinking, uncivil or disorderly recreation, or by working on that day "when absolute necessity doth not require." If one was found guilty on a third occasion of profaning the Sabbath, a public whipping could be ordered.

Members of Maryland's colonial assembly expressed great concern about the Sabbath being profaned. Attempts at a remedy eventually took the form of a second act which stated: "No person, or persons, within this province shall work or do any bodily labor, or occupation, upon any Lord's Day, commonly called Sunday, nor shall command or willfully suffer or permit of his or their children, hired servants, servants, or slaves, to work or labor as aforesaid, the absolute works of necessity and mercy always excepted."

The document went on to condemn the "wicked and profane licentiousness" of both inhabitants and travelers who customarily spent the day "in the bodily exercise or occupation of fishing," and declared such activity forthwith to be illegal.

It was likewise enacted that "no person, or persons, shall profane or abuse the said Lord's Day by drunkenness, swearing, gaming at cards, dice, billiards, shuffle board, bowls, ninepins, horse race, fowling, or hunting, or in other unlawful sports or recreation." Penalty for violating the decree was forfeiture of one hundred pounds of tobacco for each offense.

Eastern Shore violators of these blue laws included Henry Clay for cutting tobacco, Captain John Russell, a county justice, for fighting, and Edward Rogers for killing a turkey. Matthew Reed, a court commissioner, was declared guilty of a variety of misbehavior which included profaning the Sabbath by "discharging guns unseasonably."

We tend to think of Maryland as a colony where all faiths were tolerated, but you had better have a faith, and it had better be Christian. Anyone who denied that Christ was the Son of God or refuted or used reproachful words against the Holy Trinity or any of the three individuals of the Trinity could be put to death and his possessions confiscated. Reproachful remarks about the Virgin Mary, the Apostles, or the Evangelists brought only fines, whippings, and imprisonment.

It will come as no surprise, then, that an early Maryland statute made sorcery a capital offense. Anyone convicted of sorcery might be put to death or have his or her hand burnt, and could also be exiled or imprisoned for life.

The so-called Toleration Act of 1647 included little toleration for Jews. Jacob Lumbrozo, a physician of that faith, was tried on the testimony of two witnesses with uttering words of blasphemy against "Our Blessed Savior, Jesus Christ." In private conversation, Lumbrozo had indicated his belief that Jesus was just a man who accomplished his miracles by magic. Lumbrozo was tried and held over for further consideration at the next session of the provincial court. But before any decision could be reached in the Lumbrozo case, Oliver Cromwell died and was succeeded by his son Richard. In honor of the event, Josias Fendall, then governor of Maryland, pardoned and acquitted all in the province who "stood indicted, convicted, or condemned to die."

This was not Lumbrozo's only brush with the law. Once he was imprisoned on the charge of aborting the child of Elizabeth Wild, a maidservant in his employ. The baby had apparently been conceived as the result of his raping Elizabeth on numerous occasions. County commissioners referred the case to the provincial court, but the good doctor escaped trial by marrying the only witness against him, thereby disqualifying her from testifying. In another case Lumbrozo acted as attorney for two plaintiffs in a defamation suit, and is, him self, on record as filing suits against other individuals.

A number of laws were enacted for punishing drunkards. Anyone who chose to "abuse himself by frequent drunkenness" or was convicted of being drunk by the testimony of two witnesses was liable for a fine of one hundred pounds of tobacco, or, if the offender had no property, he could be imprisoned or set in stocks.

David Anderson of Talbot County successfully avoided penalties under the law by drinking himself to death. A coroner's jury, after listening to testimony and examining his body, concluded that Anderson "came to his death by being surfeited with drink." Since the verdict indicated that his departure was accidental, Anderson was granted a Christian burial.

White women who married Negro slaves were considered "forgetful of their station in life." In order to break up the practice, a law was passed in 1664 which provided that if any white woman married a Negro slave, she must serve her husband's master for as long as her spouse lived, and all children of such a marriage were bound as slaves to their father's master. This law referred only to free-born English women and did not include servants.

In 1681 another law was passed, which applied to white women servants. It declared that if the master or mistress of a white maidservant either arranged or permitted her marriage to a slave, the owner of the servant at once lost all claim to the services of the woman. Ironically, according to this statute, the servant gained her freedom by marrying a slave, and any children of the marriage were born free. In addition to losing a servant, the owner was obligated to pay a fine of ten thousand pounds of tobacco.

In early Maryland, livestock was practically a form of legal tender. Cows, oxen, hogs, sheep, and horses were exchanged in payment for a variety of services, a practice which led to much litigation.

Since livestock was generally allowed to roam at will, owners identified their animals by slitting or cutting the ears and were required to register the marks.

In 1649, after numerous complaints about hog poaching, an ordinance was enacted which provided that anyone who stole, killed, or carried away a marked swine would be required to pay double its value to the owner, two hundred pounds of tobacco to the informant, and an additional three hundred pounds to the Lord Proprietor. The same edict required anyone possessing information about hog stealing to report the facts to the constable of the hundred in which he resided. Failure to do so made an individual liable to censure and fine as the chief offender.

Residents were allowed to kill wild hogs on their property but were required to bring the ears of the slaughtered beasts together with the skin between the ears to the governor or colonial secretary within a month of the killing. The ears provided proof that the animal was not marked.

When William Price, who owned no hogs, was questioned about possessing pork, he informed authorities that it came from a wild beast, which the law allowed him to kill. Upon demand that he display the ears, Price replied that a dog had eaten them. His defense apparently failed to impress the justices. Unable to pay his fine, Price was ordered to stand in open court with a piece of paper on his chest declaring his offense and to repair a county bridge before the next meeting of the commissioners.

Hog killing and stealing continued unabated, causing the Proprietary Assembly, in 1662, to pass an additional statute providing for second offenders to have the letter "H" burned on their shoulder with a red-hot iron. Each county court was provided the necessary tool to carry out the sentence.

In 1666 the law was modified again. Anyone reputed by "common fame" to be a hog stealer, who had been warned by a planter against trespass and yet dared to hunt, risked a fine of one thousand pounds of tobacco, half of which went to the land owner and half to the Lord Proprietor. The act further provided that a first offender should stand in the pillory for four hours and then have his ears cropped. In addition, a payment of three times the value of his loss was due to the owner. Upon a second conviction the offender was to be "stigmatized" on the forehead with the letter "H." A three-time loser was declared "a felon not entitled to claim benefits of clergy."

In 1671, due to an exploding horse population, the Maryland Assembly passed an ordinance prohibiting further importation of the animals. Shortly afterward, when Talbot County resident George Robbins attempted to introduce three mares, they were confiscated.

In another case, William Sturdivant arrived on horseback from New York and had his horse seized by the sheriff. Sturdivant appealed on the grounds that he was so poor he would have to sell his clothing in order to purchase a new horse to return home. In a display of great wisdom, Talbot commissioners allowed Sturdivant to keep his mount.

From court records it would appear that colonists were either excessively concerned about their reputations or overzealous in accosting others. With only a single law on the books referring to slander, numerous suits were brought for defamation of character. The 1654 statute declared that: "All such person, or persons who, by slandering, tale bearing, or backbiting, shall scandalize the good name of any person, or persons, directly or indirectly, in such words and expressions as in the common acceptance of the English tongue, or such language as is understood, shall be counted slander, [the offender] being lawfully convicted, shall be censured both by way of satisfaction to the party injured thereby, and also for the breach of the peace."

Examples of unacceptable conduct included calling someone a "jackanape," "rascal," or "rogue." When William Price cast doubt upon Elizabeth Martin's morals, she retaliated by calling him a "perjured rogue." At trial, Mrs. Martin was fined three hundred pounds of tobacco to "repair Price's credit." Nothing is said about the comment on her morals.

When Thom South referred to Matthew Reed as a "knave,"

Reed brought an action of slander. Declared guilty, South was ordered to maintain a bridge for one year and shoulder the cost of Reed's suit.

Reed later was on the other end of litigation brought by Thomas Henson. In that proceeding Reed claimed that Henson made his living by "sharking and cozening [cheating]."

An even worse form of defamation was to accuse someone of being a thief. Talbot Commissioner Richard Wollman brought two actions against Thomas Wilkinson, first accusing the latter of injuring the commissioner's swine. The second cause was for defamation, in which Wollman claimed that Wilkinson had accused him of hog stealing. Since Wollman was a magistrate, such a remark was a reflection on his good name and "disenabled" him, the claim charged, to execute his office. At trial, Wilkinson kneeled before the court and pleaded guilty. Wollman was so pleased that he withdrew the suits.

Seth Foster, another Talbot resident, brought a successful action of defamation against Robert Knapp for spreading abroad the report that Foster was a "hog-stealing fellow from his cradle."

Proprietary officials at all levels were especially touchy about remarks which detracted from the dignity of their positions, but if the offender came publicly before them and begged forgiveness, frequently on bended knee, the abuse was generally forgiven—but not always.

When Edward Husbands, who is identified in records of the provincial assembly as a "chirurgeon" [surgeon], cursed and threatened members of the assembly, he received twenty lashes on his bare back, administered by the common hangman.

And Edward Erbery, who referred to members of the lower house as "pitiful rogues and puppies," to the house itself as "the turdy, shitten assembly," and called Charles Calvert a "rogue," suffered yet more of their wrath. Delivered before the lower house, Erbery pleaded drunkenness and was referred to the upper house, which body ordered him tied to an apple tree and publicly whipped upon his bare back with thirty-nine lashes. He was then returned to the assembly to beg forgiveness.

As an avid critic of William Donald Schaefer was heard to say, "It's a good thing for me they've changed the laws!"

∞

The man said to God, "What's a million years to you?"
And God said, "A second."
And the man said to God, "What's a million dollars to you?"
And God said, "A penny."
So the man said to God, "Will you give me a penny?"
And God said, "You'll just have to wait a second."

∞

Buzz weren't but five-foot-three, maybe, if you yanked on him real hard from both ends, an' then he weren't nothin' but breath 'n' britches besides. Many a time I heard him say to old John—old John, you know, he would go six-foot-four hunkered over. Old John would get Buzz all bent out o' shape, an' Buzz would tell him, "John, there's only one thing keeps me from punchin' you right out." I heard old Buzz say that a many a time, an' old John would just pay him no mind.

One day he told that to old John, an' I says, "Buzz, just what is it that keeps you from punchin' old John out anyway?"

Buzz looked at me, an' then he looked up at old John, an' then he looked back at me, an' he said, "Fear!"

∞

Strangers
in Our Own Land

It has been said that when the English arrived in Maryland and asked the Indians how long they had been upon the land, the first Americans replied, "We have had a Chief of Chiefs in power for thirteen generations."

As to the land itself, the natives offered legends to explain its origin. In the beginning, one such myth informs us, there was nothing but a dark, empty void. Realizing this, The Great Manitou created a very large turtle and set it in the midst of the continuum. The turtle pulled up mud and clay upon its back and formed the earth.

References to Turtle Island in ancient Indian lore are believed to refer to North America, which may be the reason that the Turtle Clan of Eastern Native Americans is generally considered to be the oldest and most respected of all the families.

I saw him just as my van reached the crest of the bridge. A steady, sharp breeze out of the northwest roiled the water below me and seemed undecided—ordering them differently with each gust—as to exactly how to arrange the long strands of his thinning hair, tied loosely in a ponytail. He paid no attention to the rattling bridge boards under my tires, but remained focused on the monofilament line which stretched from his spinning rod into the murky depths of Elliott Creek.

Sewell Winterhawk Fitzhugh is chief of the Nause-Waiwash Band of Native Americans and is usually a very busy man. I had been trying to catch up with him for months, but it was by chance that I came upon him in this rare moment of leisure. He resides less than a quarter mile from the creek.

"Anything biting?" I asked, after parking and edging in behind him on the deteriorating abutment of a former bridge.

"No, neither me nor the great heron out on the point is having much luck," he responded, nodding toward the rigid figure of a great blue heron perched on the opposite shore, where the creek skews eastward to meet Fishing Bay. "He's been there just as long as I've been here."

I wanted to talk to Fitzhugh about the history of the Nause-Waiwash (he pronounces it Nah-sue Way-wash) and the personal journey which has brought him to the honor of representing the group as chief. The name is derived from the two ancient villages to which the majority of members trace their lineage. I was unsure of how to refer to the group—should one call them a tribe, a band, or a clan?

"I'll give you a quick lesson," Fitzhugh offered, making sure I understood that the words in question represented European rather than Indian conceptions. "Tribe refers to a whole ethnically identified group of people. It has come to mean a whole nation." (Nations, in the Native American sense, I must point out, are not politically and geographically bounded in the same manner as are nations such as the United States, Mexico, Canada, etc.)

"A band," Fitzhugh instructed me, "is a group that can be identified to a certain tribe but has been separated for some reason—either by war or relocation." The Nause-Waiwash are properly referred to as a band.

Clans, I had come to understand, are branches which share some common ancestor, but with Native Americans that ancestor generally takes the form of an animal figure. The three clans from the Nanticoke Tribe that remained in Dorchester County, documented by Smithsonian records, claims Fitzhugh, were the wolf, the turkey, and the turtle clans. Fitzhugh is a member of the turtle clan and wears turtle orn-

Sewell Winterhawk Fitzhugh at Elliott Creek

aments and fetishes when dressed in native attire. He defines a clan, however, as consisting of anybody related through the maternal bloodline.

"The Nause-Waiwash," Fitzhugh continued his historical sketch, "identify with what we call the Grandfather People. These were the Lenni Lenape or what you call the Delaware. If you read the *Wallam Olum*, it talks about us separating from the Grandfather People and coming down through what is now New Jersey to Delaware Bay. Ours was a combination religious journey and practical journey. We talk of seeking out 'Sunland,' which was the eastern-most part. The East is sacred to us.

"There were three groups who had separated from the main body. One was Shawnee, and when they got to New Jersey, they went west and settled in the mountains. We and our cousins, the Piscataways, pressed south. When we hit the Delaware Bay, the enemy was behind us, and we prayed to the Grandfather, the Manitou of Manitous, and a great fog descended on the land. When the fog lifted, there was a bridge created for us, and we crossed over into what everyone now calls Delmarva. We settled here, while our cousins, the Piscataways, crossed the great tidewater bay and settled in what is now called Southern Maryland. Bands of Yoacomacoes, a part of the Piscataways, settled along the islands to keep the trade system open. Just now archeologists and historians are beginning to say, 'You know, there is some truth to these stories that the Indians have been telling us.'"

The *Wallam Olum*, also referred to as the *Red Record*, has been translated and annotated by David McCutchen and published by Avery Publishing Group, Inc. It is the epic story of the Lenni Lenape's hundred generation journey across the North American continent and is purported to be the oldest written account of a Native American people.

"The histories that were written about us after 1742," Fitzhugh continued, "refer to remnants of Nanticokes who stayed in this marsh. Some did not go north but fled out into the marsh and established homesteads."

From where we stood above the creek, we enjoyed an unob-structed view of the great marshes and bays of South Dorches-ter, outspread to the horizon across every tangent of the com-pass. In this age of mobility and crowded development it re-mains a wonderfully wild land.

"They talk about Chief Billy Rumley establishing a place on Bishops Head," Fitzhugh added. "He was originally from the village of Waiwash in the Secretary area." (Billy Rumley, pop-ular in local lore, is said to have once tied his wife to a pole and smoked her in the chimney. "To make her sweet," he is quoted as having justified his action.)

"The other village that's part of our name, Nause, was right up here," Fitzhugh said, gesturing across the marsh in the general direction of Langralls Island and the Nanticoke River.

While Waiwash is well documented, there is little historical reference to Nause. In his June to September exploration of Chesapeake Bay in 1608, Captain John Smith learned of the village but included no specific information about it in his report. It is merely a name written on a chart. Smith's map, which presents a relatively accurate picture of The Chesapeake area, contains this inscription: "Discovered and Described by Captayn [sic] John Smith—1606." The date, of course, is in-correct, as Smith did not arrive in Jamestown until May, 1607.

What Fitzhugh knows of Nause comes from the oral tradi-tion of his people, especially from stories told by his grand-mother. "The Nanticoke people who moved north talked about Nause, and there are other references. We know there were three clans left out of that village."

"Does anyone know the location?" I asked, feeling certain that the answer would be negative.

"Yes," came the surprise response.

"Can you say where it is?"

"No!"

Fitzhugh's reply was terse but delivered with a smile.

"For years the state used to say it was at a certain place,

but it isn't, never was, and it never will be. They had a sign out on the Nanticoke River one time. It said, 'Believed to be the site of the village of Nause.'"

Pointing to a barely visible, hazy smudge on the horizon across Fishing Bay, Fitzhugh changed the subject. "The last longhouse of my people sat on that island—Snake Island. It was the last in my direct bloodline. On this side, facing Fishing Bay, sat the longhouse. On the other side sat an English-style home—the plantation house. It was in existence into the eighteenth century. The island is washing away terribly; there's not much left. You can still see bricks where the English house stood, and on a real low tide you can find the fire pits out in the water where the longhouse was. I've heard my grandmother say that there was a peach orchard on the island when she was a little girl. There are several others who remember when there were still fields there, and people from the other side of Fishing Bay would plant plots there, especially cantaloupes and watermelons.

"I did my last vision quest on Snake Island," Fitzhugh said with what I thought might be a slight touch of nostalgia in his voice. "I spent four days there by myself, just before I became chief several years ago."

"Was the quest successful?" I wanted to know, a little unsure of how to phrase the question or whether it was even proper to inquire about something so personal.

"Well, I learned a lot," Fitzhugh sighed, "if that's what you consider successful. The European way of considering success and our way. . . ." He paused for a moment, then said, "I had a cousin leave the county about twenty years ago. He found it too difficult to stay here and maintain his Indian identity, so he cleaned up and moved out to the Wind River Indian Reservation; although," Fitzhugh chuckled—a strand of hair whipping around into his face—"I think sometimes we have more wind here. My cousin is very happy. He likes it out there. But a lot of us don't want to leave, even though it's getting harder here."

I directed the conversation back to the matter of what

constitutes success in his view.

"I think European society bases too much on having a title and on having money. For Native Americans it's very hard to . . . what we call 'live in both worlds.' We realize, those of us who are realistic, that we have to have money to live, and that seems to get scarcer for us around here every year. But our first concern is how we stand in the eyes of the creator.

"The more corrupt a man is in white society, the higher, it seems, he can go. Among Native Americans you prove yourself —it's not assumed. You don't sit on your haunches. I find the older I get, the more traditional I get, and I find it very hard dealing with the outside world at times. Some years ago I had a review where I was working. One of my supervisors looked at me and told me that if I didn't learn how to lie, I wasn't going to get anywhere. And the Christian teaches in church, 'Thou shalt not lie.' I tried it one time. I was young: eighteen, nineteen, twenty—somewhere in there. These people I was dealing with were very hard people to deal with. I told one lie and had to tell another to cover that lie up. Then I had to tell another to cover that up. The next thing I knew, I was in so deep.

"My grandmother was my first teacher and a good one. Before she'd lie to you, she'd put her head down and not say anything.

"I call things the way they are. Maybe the way I see something is not the way somebody else sees it, but if you tell it from here (he touched his hand to his chest), you ain't got to worry about it."

A car rumbled onto the bridge and paused. "Go on up to the house," Fitzhugh called to its passengers, "I'll be right there." Reeling in his line and turning to me, he explained, "Those are my guests; I have to go now."

As if on cue, the great blue heron lifted from its sentinel post near the mouth of the creek and winged low and slowly across the marsh toward the Nanticoke River. "Well, he's giving up too," observed Fitzhugh. "He couldn't find anything either."

We shook hands and agreed to talk again.

Three months passed after our chance encounter at Elliott Creek before Sewell Winterhawk Fitzhugh and I had another opportunity to talk.

"I never catch up anymore," he said with a sigh; "it's just constantly tread."

"You've chosen a busy life," I acknowledged.

"I didn't ask for it; it just came my way."

There are, by Fitzhugh's estimation, more than five thousand individuals in the region with Native American bloodlines. The Nause-Waiwash have an active enrollment of about two hundred.

"Another four hundred," said Fitzhugh, "use the tribal office. Tonight, for instance, I handled a call from a Seminole family that has renting problems."

"Are you tied in with other groups?" I asked.

"What do you mean by 'tied in?'" Fitzhugh chuckled—"Telegraph?"

"Do you have relationships with other groups?" I tried to clarify my question.

"Yes," Fitzhugh acknowledged. "Each group has its own sovereignty, but there are issues that the groups work on together, such as recognition, education, and reparations—returning ceremonial items and the remains of our ancestors. We try to help each other. I appeared in front of the Maryland Commission of Indian Affairs on the first of this month, and I've been working with archaeologists at Chicone, our ancient chief-of-chief's village north of Vienna. We deal a lot with other tribes. I don't like to give details, but, for example, we had a Cherokee woman here who needed assistance. We got in touch with the tribal office in North Carolina and were able to help her return home. And other ethnic communities will use the office at times. We deal with everything from alcoholism to AIDS to drugs. We try to help where we can, but it's a full-time job."

"I'm not sure I understand exactly what you mean by your 'tribal office.'"

"The office for the Nause-Waiwash Band of Indian People," replied Fitzhugh, "runs out of one room in our house. It used to be half of our living room when we lived in Cambridge."

"Do you have any direct contact," I wondered, "with the Nanticokes of Indian River in Delaware?"

"We often work together," Fitzhugh said. "We won back the remains of forty some of our ancestors from the state. They are now buried over at Wesley Methodist Church in Andrews, Maryland. But the state makes hoops for you to jump through. 'What happens,' they asked us, 'if the group in Delaware lays claim to the remains?' So we went over and visited with the Nanticoke council, and they gave us a letter saying they would handle the Delaware side of the line and support us to handle the Maryland side. Chief Clark [Nanticoke] and the Yhough-hegheny Band of Shawnees both gave letters supporting us."

"I know there are other native American remains still in the state's custody," I acknowledged. "What progress is being made to recover them?"

"It's slow; it will always be slow," Fitzhugh sighed. "You have some who are far-visioned enough, and they know the tide is turning, that eventually all the remains are going to have to be returned. But you also have people in the right places who say, 'No, we're not going to do this.' How would you like to have your grandmother shoved in . . . ?"

He did not finish the sentence.

"What's the state doing with the remains?" I asked.

"Nothing."

"Why do you think they continue to hold them?"

"A woman in Annapolis once told me," replied Fitzhugh, "that they find us Native Americans to be a 'cute little ethnic curiosity.'"

"Do I understand correctly that Maryland has never extended official recognition to your band?"

"Officially," Fitzhugh acknowledged, "Maryland has not recognized any of its Native American groups. Unofficially, they will concede that they know they have Native Americans living in Maryland. And the Feds do it too. The Feds have what they call 'fully recognized tribes,' and they have others that are not fully recognized, but they acknowledge their existence. Then they have some that were recognized fully, which they decided they aren't going to fully recognized any longer. They also have what they call 'state recognized' and 'unofficially state recognized.' Do you see what I'm saying?"

I changed the subject. "I'd like to talk a little more about the colonial period and what led to the exodus of most Native Americans from Delmarva. How bad did things get?"

"Remember the phrase," Fitzhugh answered with a question of his own, "'The only good Indian is a dead Indian?' It was coined right here on the Eastern Shore. It came from a high sheriff by the name of Scarborough. He was known to our people as a conjure. He sent letters out to plantation owners: 'Look, you have an Indian problem, and you need slaves. If you come upon an Indian household, you have my permission to kill the men and boys of age and breed the women and children with your African stock. In that way we can do away with the Indian problem, and you can get free slaves.' It's one of the reasons that a lot of us are triracially and not just biracially mixed."

Although he owned some land in Maryland, it will always be a mystery why Governor Charles Calvert chose Colonel Edmund Scarborough of Accomack, Virginia, to serve as a commissioner for the Eastern Shore. Scarborough was an ardent Virginian and a notorious enemy of the Indian.

On one occasion, annoyed by some minor pilfering on his plantation, the colonel invited neighboring natives to gather in a ditch, where, he promised, the Great Spirit would speak to them. The Great Spirit turned out to be a concealed cannon.

Many Pocomokes were slashed to death in a saber charge led by Scarborough, and with the help of smallpox he wiped out the gentle Assateagues.

In spite of Calvert's concession to him, Scarborough raided the governor's colony from Virginia and once attempted to annex much of Somerset County. A Pocomoke chief is credited with saying this about him:

> In the moon of the roasting ears, palefaces from the land of the Accomacs wanted war. The black wampum belt with the red hatchet painted on it was sent from chief to chief along the seaside and over beyond Pocomoke. The King [Scarborough] of the bad whites was angry and came with horse and guns. After a while the cloud went down. The Quackels [Quakers] came into our land. The bad white chief and his friends had driven them out. They loved peace. But one time he put on his war paint and swam the rivers and followed them. He hated Quackels. The Quackels were kind to Indians. Then the great father across the Bay said the bad white chief must stay beyond the marked trees.

Scarborough, in fact, isolated from the administrative centers of both Virginia and Maryland, suffered little effective challenge to his outrageous conduct.

"By 1742," continued Fitzhugh, "after Tecumseh's attempt to unite us all and drive the Europeans into the sea, we knew we were whipped. We became, as my grandmother used to say, 'strangers in our own land.' That's when the great exodus began.

Many migrated north to join the Iroquois. They were enemies of ours, but better an enemy you could understand than one you couldn't comprehend. Those who stayed fled into the marsh. The Europeans wanted the high land to plant tobacco and cotton. The marsh gave us enough land to grow the crops we needed, and we had the trapping and the fish and the oyster.

"George Thomas Stewart is a white ancestor of mine. He was part of the militia which was supposed to attack us in the last war they declared on us in 1742, but he turned around and married one of our women. Go back and read the history. Claiborne was married to an Indian; that's how he laid claim to

Kent Island. She was the daughter of a chief. By marrying her it made him heir. It boiled down to land."

As part of their quest for formal recognition, the Nause-Waiwash have made concessions to modern business and government and have become incorporated.

"We have bylaws," Fitzhugh told me, "but much is based on the old traditions."

"And how were you selected as chief?" I wanted to know.

"When our people decided to reestablish the hereditary chief lines, they decided to do it in the traditional way, which is to have the women decide—all the enrolled women of age."

"And what does 'of age' mean?"

"When they start the time of the moon."

"Is it a majority rule?"

"It should be a consensus."

"How long is the chief's term?"

"Traditionally, a chief is chief for as long as the people choose to follow him. When the people no longer feel that the chief does the will of the people, the women get together again. We have elections every four years for Council. We have a seven-member council."

"In addition to what most people would call your 'Christian name,' you use an Indian name, 'Winterhawk,'" I observed. "How did you acquire that?"

"It was given to me."

"Given to you? How?" I pressed.

"It was given to me on my first vision quest by the Creator."

"How would you describe a vision quest to someone who knows nothing about the subject?"

"Most people," Fitzhugh began, "think it is something that happens in one or two days. It doesn't. I was a young man, and my dad had just had his first heart attack. We moved back down to Andrews. I went to my grandmother and wanted to learn, and she agreed to teach me. Of the five grandchildren, I was the only one who had any interest. For about two years she worked with me, talked about the old legends and the way

Chief Fitzhugh in Native American Attire

things were done. When I felt I was ready, I went back to what was called Mildred's Woods, my grandmother's woods, and it was there that I got my name that Sunday morning. That's as far as I'm going to go."

At the intersection of Green Brier and Maple Dam Roads in Dorchester County, a small frame building stands in a serious state of disrepair. This Nineteenth Century structure, which has served Native Americans and more recently African Americans as meeting hall and chapel, is now intended as the longhouse of the Nause-Waiwash. It represents an elusive dream which may soon achieve reality.

As we prepared to part, I asked Sewell Winterhawk Fitzhugh one final question: "What haven't we discussed that you would like others to understand about your people, your interests, and your dreams?"

"We are as versatile as any other people," he said without a second's hesitation. "When I went to my grandmother and wanted to learn, I felt the old ways were going to die forever. That's one of the reasons I wanted to learn. But what I've seen happen in the last twenty years is not the dying of a people, but the rebirth of a people. I have seen a people, who for generations had been taught to be ashamed of being Indian or part Indian, learn to hold their heads up and be proud of it. Listening to people and putting it all together like a big puzzle gives you a beautiful picture of how we survived.

"There are so many stories. We found out who the last potter was among our people. I got a phone call from a man in Florida who is one of our people. He had this woman's rubbing stones. On her deathbed she gave them to her nephew, and he took them to Florida with him. He brought them back so we could take pictures of them.

"Some of the stories are amazing. I've had people talk about dealing with the 'sheet people.' You would call them the KKK. One woman in her seventies talked about how, when she was a young girl, it was worse being an Indian than it was being black—and they shot black people back then.

"I've seen people grow very proud, but the only way we can heal completely is to learn that we're all in it together. It doesn't matter what the color of the skin is, the ethnic background—whatever. We have a beautiful history, and we have to look at that history for what it can teach us and then go on.

"My number one dream is to see the longhouse up and functioning. I'm not going to live forever, I know that—don't want to—but I want to be able, when I cross the veil, to know that my people are going to survive as a people."

∞

This boy used to hang around the store, and Mr. Jim would let him sweep the floor or somethin' for a piece of pie or a san'-wich. He couldn't get no regular job. One day a feller in there said, "Eddie, which would you rather have, this nice shiny penny here, or this little dime?"

"I'd like the penny," says Eddie.

Well, all the boys thought that was pretty funny, and it got so whenever they wanted a laugh, they would ask Eddie which he wanted—a penny or a dime.

One day a fella from the city come in there, and he didn't like the way the boys was foolin' old Eddie. He took the boy outside and told him, "Son, these men are takin' advantage of you. You kin get ten pennies for a dime. Next time they offer you a penny or a dime, you take the dime?"

"I don't wanna do that, sir," Eddie says.

"Why not?" the man says. "I just told you, you can get ten pennies for every dime you have."

"But if I take the dime," says Eddie, "they won't ask me no more."

∞

A Small Green Plant

"**Y**ou go on down to Gumboro Store," Eddie West advised me; "that's where it happens." Then he added with a grin, "Of course some of the boys might mess with you a little. I had one guy in there tell me he had a moose down in that swamp. He swore by a Bible about that."

The Gumboro General Store was built on the opposite side of Delaware Route 30 from its present location, "But it was a store even when it was on the other side of the road," I was told one day when I stopped for lunch. "They pulled it across with oxen in 1926. My dad remembers it." Then in the same breath my informant added, "When it's windy and cold outside, it's just as warm in here as it can be."

While I was pondering the relationship of those tidbits of information, someone else nodded to a gentleman savoring a ham and cheese sandwich and announced, "His father owned the store one time, and his uncle owned it too."

And if I understood correctly, the parents as well as an aunt and uncle of the wife of the present proprietor occupied it some fifty years ago. The history of the Gumboro General Store would appear to be a complexity of interrelationships, and with a multitude of survivors who continue as patrons. In fact, a former holder of the deed was also present. "We didn't keep it very long," was her only contribution to the conversation.

The gentleman with the ham and cheese changed the subject: "They play Rook in here at night," he said. "All day if it rains."

"I've seen a lot of things go though here in forty years," an old timer declared.

A conversation at the next table was hard to ignore: "Headless cabbage," the middle-aged chap who worked at a nearby sawmill observed with a sober nod, "that's good stuff. It's a little tough to find seed though."

"Seedless watermelons too!" a man in coveralls added with an equally sincere demeanor.

Eddie West was right, you just might get messed with a little in the Gumboro Store.

I decided it was time to pop the question I had come to ask: "Have you ever seen or heard the wampus?" I directed my query to the man who was expounding the virtues of headless cabbage.

"He's too young for the wampus," the old timer answered instead. "In his time it was the swamp monster, but come to find out, this boy lived up there through the swamp, and he was dressin' up like a monster. It was in the news and in the papers. He'd jump in front of cars comin' through there—lucky thing he didn't get hisself killed or shot or somethin'—then he'd run back in the swamp."

"Is that guy still around?" I wanted to know.

"Oh, he's around fifty year old now—lives through the swamp on the other side. Go through; take the first left; make another left. Can't miss it. He works in a clothin' store in Selbyville."

Stories about the wampus—sometimes referred to as the burnt monster—go back nearly a century, and most seem to have originated in the Gumboro area. Some believe the wampus is, or was, a mountain lion which lived in the Cypress Swamp, a sprawling wilderness of ten thousand acres directly east of Gumboro. There are also stories of area farmers hearing noises at night and encountering horrible creatures.

And there is the legend of the hook man, a hermit with a hook for a hand, who lived in Cypress Swamp. I had been told a story about a young couple who suffered a flat tire one night while traveling through the barrens. "Before he walked out for help, the boy instructed his girlfriend to stay in the car and lock the doors. She was sitting there in the dark, when suddenly there was a sharp tap, tap, tap on the window."

"What happened then?" I had asked the teller, when she concluded the tale at that suspenseful point.

"I don't know; that's all I heard," was her deflating reply.

I repeated the unfinished story in the Gumboro Store and looked around for some sign of recognition.

"Hookman, huh?" a customer who had just polished off a cheeseburger and plate of fries pondered. "Didn't Johnny Phillips have a hook? That's been fifty years ago."

Disappointingly, the crowd's interest in swamp monsters and hookmen ended as abruptly as the story I had been told.

Behind me, three customers were engaged in a discussion about the directions someone on television had given to get from Millsboro to Gumboro. "He said it was nine miles west from Millsboro. Now that's not the direction to my thinkin'."

"Well, if he ain't never been here, he'll learn somethin' before he leaves," a tall gentleman soberly proclaimed as he, himself, rose to leave.

From two tables away a young man in jeans and red shirt observed the departure and hooted, "Hey Birdlegs, where you goin'?"

Birdlegs was headed back to work.

The man across the table had finished his sandwich. "I'll tell you a story that involved a country store and a sixteen-year-old colored boy," he said quietly.

I gave him my complete attention.

"Not here," he responded. "I've got to be where it happened to tell it. Have you got a few minutes to take a ride?"

I did.

We headed east from Gumboro toward Cypress Swamp. Along the way my guide pointed to a neatly kept farmhouse and said, "The woman who lives right here called her brother-in-law the other night and said for him to come over. 'A fox has got my cat up a tree,' she told him. He come on over, and there was that fox, settin' there barkin' at her cat.

"After you get around this curve here, I want you to pull up in the road just on this side of that mailbox. Pull up by that woods and I'll show you what I'm talkin' about and tell you the story. Right here is where the swamp begins. Water," he said, gesturing into the thicket, "used to stand in there all the time. I've come right down here, and you could just hear bullfrog after bullfrog after bullfrog in there. You know a bullfrog will cry just like a baby."

I didn't know.

"I can hide in that bush with a bullfrog, and I can have people lookin' for a baby in there, just by ticklin' that thing on the belly. Take him from the back; turn him up; take a feather or somethin' real soft and just tickle him."

I peered into the swamp's green lushness. Even in the midst of the drought we were experiencing, the terrain was damp, and small pools glistened here and there in the gloom, but there were no bullfrogs garumping—or crying either.

"The story starts in 1910," my narrator continued. "I went backward from the years he stayed with my family, and it had to be then if all the figures are right. There was a store right here—right in there—and if you go down the road about eight-tenths of a mile and then turn left and go up into the swamp, there's a place called Ten Foot. That's where my father and mother moved off to when they got married—housekeepin'.

"My father happened to be down here to the store one Saturday afternoon, and this colored boy come in, and he had three cents in his pocket. He wanted to know if he could buy some cakes or whatever he could get for three cents, and the local boys wanted to run him off. My father said, 'No, you leave him alone. He ain't hurtin' you, so don't bother him.' That had to be in the spring or the summer of the year of 1910.

"So after the boy got his cakes, my father asked him did he have a place to stay. The boy said, 'No,' and my father said, 'Well, come on up to my house, and I'll make a place for you out in the barn.' So he did, and the boy stayed that night.

"When my father and mother got up the next mornin', the boy had fed the team, milked the cow, pumped the water—had all the chores done.

"My parents didn't have much worth stealin' back then. My father told my mother, 'We'll find out what he's like. We'll put a couple dollars on the table and leave the door open, and we'll go some place.' So that's what they done; they went over to my grandfather's.

"When they come back on Sunday afternoon, the boy had repeated the whole chores. My father seen that he wanted to do a decent thing, so he asked him if he would like to stay. The boy said yes, he would like that. When he came, he was barefooted. After he said he would stay, my father brought him down here to the store and bought him clothes and shoes.

"So my father took him in, just as one of the children. He stayed right in the house with us, and he eat at the same table with us. He treated my father and mother like they were saints to him.

"He would get up four o'clock in the mornin', have all the fires goin', the house heated and all; then he'd go out and feed the team, milk the cow, bring the wood in. You could work right side of him all day long, and he would never say a word to you. If you asked him a question, he would answer it: 'Charles, ain't you cold?' 'Just a little chilly,' is all he would say, and he'd go right back to work.

"He didn't have any education that we ever knew of. The best we could find about him, his name was Charles Henry Henderson, and he was originally from Snow Hill. I've often wondered if I could go down there and find any of his family. He claimed only a little bit about himself. His stepfather beat him bad; that's about all he would say.

"He made it easy for my parents, and he done that for twenty-four years until he died. He died in that house right there [the old man pointed toward an abandoned structure across the field]. My parents had moved here after a while. He died up in the second story on this back corner. He had a stroke, and when he tried to get up, he fell back. His head was to that window there. It was on a Saturday night, and he died Sunday about twelve o'clock. He was forty years old and had spent twenty-four years with my parents.

"When he passed away, my father had a colored choir come from Millsboro. They sang in that house there, and a colored preacher preached the sermon. He's buried just beyond that old building. If you want to pull around there, I can show you. There ain't nobody lives here now; ain't nobody gonna bother us. I know the people that owns it."

As we inched our way down the overgrown lane, tall grasses already gone to seed brushed the underside of my van. Two turkey vultures, wings tilted, circled lazily in the shimmering, pale-blue summer sky.

"Stop here," my guide instructed as we came to a large, rectangular, flat-topped mound of earth. Throughout the Delmarva Peninsula, where water tables are historically high, raised burial grounds are not uncommon.

"They moved most of the people that was in this cemetery and carried 'em somewheres else and reburied 'em," the man said as we circled on foot around the hillock, passing three well-worn entrances to a fox den. "I don't know whether I can find his grave or not. The last time I was back here, his vault was busted out at one end. If it had done him any good, I would have made the whole thing over, but when a person's dead, they're dead; you can't help 'em a bit."

We passed a collection of bleached bones—deer, we determined.

"I've found a lot of arrowheads around here," the man said, and then we came upon a single vault, its end "busted out." A ray of sunlight slanted down into the crypt, creating a bright ring on the rust-tinted earth inside. And there, in the center of the circle of golden light, amid a scattering of brown, moldering bones, a single, small, luxuriously-green plant had taken root and was reaching for the sky.

∞

The Hermit of Puckum

Between Hurlock and Finchville, Route 392 spans Marsh-yhope Creek on the Harrison Ferry Bridge. As its name suggests, the river crossing was once made by scow. On the east bank one enters a region generally referred to as Puckum. Older residents can remember a time when it was densely forested and visited primarily by cord-wood cutters and hunters. In some parts the scenery has changed little, the land remaining largely covered with a tangle of vegetation.

I was discussing Puckum with a gentleman whose family has lived there for generations, when he said, "On up from Harrison Ferry, toward Federalsburg, there used to be an old hermit by the name of Sam Bull lived in a cave back there."

Of course I was immediately fascinated.

"He lived in a hole in the ground," my informant continued. "It was just about wide enough for his bed and a little table. I've been in there when I was a kid. The cave had a tin roof on it."

"How did he make a living?" I wanted to know.

"He had fish ponds dug back there, and he raised his own fish. When the tide would come up, he'd open some boards in a ditch and let the water in. He'd put 'em back down again when the tide went out, and the water would stay in there.

"Bull left out of here a long time ago and went to Texas. This is hearsay, now, but they say his brother died and left him the rights to six oil wells. After he left, we used to go bullfroggin' in them ponds. If we can still get back in there,

I'll show you where it's at."

Since the Delmarva summer was approaching with a vengeance, we agreed to meet in Puckum after the mosquito, fly, and tick seasons had ended, but Lee Harper died before the leaves fell that year.

My curiosity did not allow Sam Bull to rest for very long, and I began to make inquiries of other residents around the communities of Hurlock, Williamsburg, and Federalsburg. It did not take long to realize that Sam Bull had become a legend and that the truth was going to be elusive.

"Sam Bull," another local pondered, "he's been dead a hundred years, ain't he? He used to live there to Harrison Ferry, did he? Years ago that's all you'd hear about: 'Old Sam Bull lives back in there by hisself.' People were near'bout afraid to go back there."

"Do you know what he did for a living?" I asked.

"He didn't do nothin', I don't think," came the quick reply, to which was added the afterthought: "I remember he walked there to Williamsburg years ago to get his groceries. That's when I was just a little, teeny tot."

"During the war [1941-1945]," my next contact, an octogenarian, offered, "he still lived back in that thicket of Puckum. You're way back from anywhere when you're in there. In a way it's not that far, but you're in the thicket, and Bull lived back to the river. I don't remember him ever having a woman in there. From what I gather, he was a unique kind of guy. My only trip in there was in a truck to get some gravel. That would have been in 1934 or '35. He had a small gravel pit, and there was a little bit of land to till. During the war it was questionable that maybe he was some kind of a spy. There was talk that he had a short-wave radio, and he'd travel by night on the river in his boat. I never heard how he got here or why anyone would go way back there to live."

"The Bull tract," former Hurlock mayor Winfield Trice told me, "was the most beautiful tract you ever saw. It was about forty acres of rolling land and woods, and then you came down to the river where the house was. The thing that impressed me the most was all his contraptions—ditches and little guts. The story was that the tide would come in and bring fish with it. He'd lower a piece of wood which made a dam, and then he didn't have to work for his fish. Obviously he was an eccentric man. I never saw him, and I can't tell you anything about the man himself."

A woman in Federalsburg advised me: "He wasn't very friendly, and people were afraid of him, but the boys used to go back there and rabbit hunt, and he was never unkind to them. He would talk to them some, but if he didn't want to talk, he would send them on their way. We were never sure just how he made his living; we wondered if maybe he didn't have a still. The only place anybody ever saw him was at Bailey's Store."

My conversations with people who were supposed to have known Sam Bull have frequently developed like this exchange, which I take directly from my notes:

"Did you ever go back to where he lived?"

"I've been back there many a time."

"What did his house look like?"

"I really couldn't tell you."

"What did he look like?"

"Well, I can't really say after all this time."

"Did he have friends?"

"I don't know if he did or not."

"What happened to him?"

"I don't know what ever happened to him."

"Why did he live back there?"

"I guess he was crazy."

"What did he do for a living?"

"God only knows. I never seen the man work."

"But you did see him?"

"Oh yeah, I seen him many times."

Almost everyone I spoke to agreed, as one gentleman put it, that "Sam Bull had funny ways," to which he then added,

"Anybody that would go around him—if he seen 'em comin' —they never would find him."

Bull's residence remains a mystery to me, having been described as everything from a cave or mostly subterranean cubicle to a shack or a small house of normal appearance.

As for Sam Bull himself: "Well, he was a big, robust fellow," is the best portrait most can conjure up.

The only detailed characterization of the man was delivered to me in a telephone conversation with Marty Harper: "He was about five-foot-seven and weighed about a hundred and eighty-five pounds. I don't think he ever had a razor, but someone would shave him now and then. He had a big huntin' knife he carried on his belt.

"He always walked with two sticks—they were more like poles—and he had three black dogs he always carried with him. People in them days would use sticks to help you walk along—to give you a boost. You ever see a killdee [killdeer] walkin'? Well, that's the way Bull walked, with a stick in each hand, and his hands would be dern near straight out from his shoulders. He'd come through that woods better'n a motorcycle could.

"In them days everybody was just scared of him. You didn't come on his land. I believe you could walk in there pitch dark at night, and when you stepped across his line with one foot, he'd be facin' you. He had a set of ears on him that a microscope couldn't think of.

"He came out of Texas, and he owned a whole bunch of oil wells down there, and that's where he went down to die, finally. I'll say it in plain English: in them days everybody killed everybody, and when they got blamed, they just disappeared. They'd go to places, and Sam Bull came this way.

"He built himself an underground house back there."

"Can you describe it?" I asked.

"You're talkin' years now. I'd say about ten foot wide, about fifteen foot long, and it was buried underground with logs on top of it. It was just an underground house, and he had a big well dug outside of it. Marshyhope Creek was real clean then, and he had ditches dug out from it which run water into the well. He had a bunch of wells. One he had was just like a spring; it would sit there and boil—the sand would.

"In the depression in the thirties, the government had all these people come and dig ditches. They were drainin' the marshes and everything else. We had the WPA and the CCC camps. There were three of 'em around here. And then in the war they had all the prisoners from Germany diggin' ditches too. Sam Bull had 'em diggin' over to where he lived. He had them ditches dug so he could trap fish and crawfish. He would run rock[fish] into one ditch and fence 'em off and raise 'em into it. And other ones, like catfish, he'd run into the CCC ditch. He had it where he didn't have to fish really all winter long.

"He had like pyramids built where he kept different things. He had everything buried. Where the old house was, there's still one mound of dirt. I've been plannin' for years to go dig it. I know he's got somethin' in it, but I don't know what.

"For a while he worked in a hardware store. He would walk all the way clear to Federalsburg and back.

"He had like a raft which he poled on the river, and he had a bridge under water right to his house. You could drive a horse and wagon across, and you could walk across there waist deep.

"There's four bridges on the creek where you can walk a-cross and go across with horses. These didn't have no bridges like Harrison Ferry; they were bridges under water. They took sand and oyster shell and dumped 'em overboard till they got it shallow enough where a horse and wagon could go a-cross. One was off of Brown's Wharf and another about three miles up river.

"Bull had a daughter in Texas. When he went back there, he went into an old-age home, and she took care of him. He sold his oil wells, and then he just died. I can't remember the name of the town now where he's buried.

"If you want to go and see how it was laid over, you have to walk through there after the leaves are gone; then you can see somethin'. Of course it's all growed up now, but they still haven't changed the ditches or where he had dams. It's all still there; you just have to know where it's at."

If Sam lived on Bull's Point today, his nearest neighbor would be Lloyd Fooks, who built his home a short distance upriver in 1969. "When I was four or five years old," Fooks told me, "I spent part of a day at his house. I vaguely remember what it looked like; it was a regular farm house but not very large. He lived like a hermit back there, but it was comfortable living in a sense. He had everything neatly laid out." Fooks estimates that Bull has been gone from the point for nearly fifty years.

Amy Fooks, Lloyd's daughter, visited Bull's' Point when she was a child and remembers an old, rotted wooden boat on the shore and what she calls his refrigerator. From her description it appears to have been an old-fashioned root cellar dug into the side of a dirt mound. "The Boy Scouts used to camp there," she told me. "Maybe they still do."

The Bull tract, as many old-timers still refer to it, was purchased by The Chesapeake Corporation of Virginia, a timber company. On a hot afternoon in late spring, with sheep flies buzzing orbits around my perspiring head, I ignored a "No Trespassing" sign and utilized one of Chesapeake's service roads to approach the point. The ribbon of sand traversed a ridge forested with loblolly pines and vibrant with songs of chickadees and wood thrushes.

As the range fell away toward the river, my passageway narrowed, and I was forced to push through a tangle of gum and maple saplings stitched with briar. Once through the wall of green I stumbled across the remains of another road—little more than a suggestion on the forest floor—and followed it toward a brightness which I correctly assumed to be open sky above the river. A short walk brought me to a fire pit, several rough benches, and a table—the Boy Scout camp Amy Fooks had mentioned.

You might say that Bull's Point is divided into three parts by a pair of shallow, silted streams, replete with scurrying minnows. Along each of the runs lies a well-settled berm, evidence that shovels were at work there many years ago. Two nondescript mounds of earth offer no hint of their original function. The garumping of bullfrogs resonated from a small pond nestled in the woods a hundred yards behind the point.

Leaning against a tree next to the Marshyhope, I stood for a few long, idle moments, absorbing the view across a deep bend bursting with the lush green of tuckahoe and a golden afternoon haze. Had I first experienced the serenity of Bull's Point, I never would have asked why he chose to live there.

Was Sam Bull a murderer? Perhaps. Was Sam Bull crazy? I don't think so.

Postscript

In April, 1999, Chesapeake Forest Products agreed to sell 278,000 acres to a timber subsidiary of John Hancock Mutual Life Insurance Company, and in the fall of the same year the state of Maryland purchased 58,000 acres of the Chesapeake property, primarily forest and wetland within the Nanticoke River watershed. Bull's Point was included in the package.

∞

If you have warts on your hand, they used to say, you should steal somebody's dish rag, and they'll go away.

∞

The Other Hal Roth

This story begins nearly twenty years ago, when I arrived home one evening, exhausted from a long and trying day of administering to the affairs of a large public high school. I was hoping to savor a brief nap before dinner, but those intentions were quickly turned aside by a knock on my front door. Opening it, I encountered a UPS driver who appeared even more fatigued than I.

"Are you Hal Roth," he asked, his voice edged, I thought, with a tone of apprehension, as though he anticipated and dreaded a negative answer.

"I am," I replied.

His weariness echoed in every word. "You're a hard man to find," he said.

"Oh, Really?" I protested. "I work in a high school which serves two thousand students, four thousand parents, and employs a hundred and twenty-five teachers, and not one of them has a bit of trouble locating me day or night."

But the only reply from the man in the brown uniform was to hand me a heavy box and disappear into the gathering dusk.

I lugged the parcel to a table, curiously noting that it was from W. W. Norton Company, book publishers, and slit the tape securing the top flaps. When I folded them back, I was confronted by the dust jacket of a book. The cover photograph depicted a tiny sailing vessel, almost lost in the depths of a fjord, dwarfed by towering walls of granite over which multi-

ple waterfalls cascaded from a crowning glacier. It was a majestic scene. The book's title, in sunny yellow print, shouted
"*Two Against Cape Horn*," but it was the bold red of the auth-
or's name which caught and riveted my attention: "Hal Roth."

I was tired, and my mind was a bit fuzzy, but I felt pretty
damned sure I hadn't written it. I turned the flaps down again
and read the label for the first time. The carton was addressed simply to: "Hal Roth (in care of a name which I have forgotten), Annapolis, Maryland." I was living in Glen Burnie at
the time, fourteen miles north of Maryland's capitol.

That evening I checked the phone books and worried several operators without success. There was no internet in those
years to assist with people searches. I made additional calls
the following day and spoke with a variety of individuals
whom I hoped might provide assistance in getting the ship-
ment to its proper owner. No luck!

Several weeks later, the box of books still in my study, a
teacher introduced me to two men who had been invited to
speak to our science classes. "Hal Roth?" responded one of the
guests, Are you related to the sailor Hal Roth?"

"No," I replied, "but I certainly would like to know where
he is at the moment."

"That's easy," the gentleman smiled. "*Whisper* is tied up
in Annapolis at such-and-such boat yard."

Whisper was the thirty-five-foot yacht in which Hal and
his wife, Margaret, had sailed from California, traveling eight
thousand miles around Cape Horn to the East Coast. Twenty-
four miles from the bottom of the world they had been shipwrecked in a violent storm and were rescued by a Chilean
navy patrol boat. It was the adventure which had spawned
the box of books.

It did not take me long to call the boat yard. "Hal and
Margaret just left," a friendly voice informed me, "but they'll
be back later, and they have a phone on the yacht."

That evening we talked. The books had been ordered for
an event and had been replaced when they went astray to my

address. I received an invitation to visit with Hal and Margaret on Whisper, but my days were bulging with work and commitments. The weeks moved on, and I never called back.

I became involved in editing and publishing a small literary journal and one day received a letter from a reader in California: "I've been wondering where you got to. I've been trying to find you." I had to inform the woman that her search had not ended, that I had no idea where Hal and Margaret Roth might be. Then a man wrote from Maine, another from somewhere else. I could only suggest that they contact W. W. Norton and hope their letters would be forwarded.

Over the years I encountered additional books written by the other Hal Roth. *Two on a Big Ocean* and *After 50,000 Miles* had preceded his Book-of-the-Month-Club selection, *Two Against Cape Horn.* In 1983 *The Longest Race* was added to Hal's credits, followed by *Always a Distant Anchorage*, *Chasing the Long Rainbow*, and *Chasing the Wind.*

Eventually I retired and moved to the Eastern Shore, to a tree farm which had served as a weekend retreat since 1972. After completing construction of a new home there, I turned my attention to gathering stories and writing about the people and lore of Delmarva. Not long after I published my first collection of anecdotes, a bookstore manager called and invited me to a signing. She informed me that she had first checked her phone book and called the number listed there for Hal Roth.

"Will you do a signing for us?" she had asked.

"Certainly," came the reply. "Which book do you want me to sign?"

"*Conversations In A Country Store.*"

"Well," her party offered after a moment's hesitation, "we have a problem. I didn't write that book."

And that was how I came to discover that Hal Roth, accomplished mariner and author of some of our finest books about sailing, had also chosen an anchorage on Maryland's Eastern Shore.

Since then, on both sides of the bay and in Delaware, the

other Hal's fans have appeared at my events, sometimes with quizzical looks clouding their expressions—they had seen his picture, and I just didn't match. Once I spotted a woman approaching from across the room, clutching, I believe, nearly every volume he has written. Most graciously, she did not display what had to be her disappointment and generously added a book of mine to the top of her pile.

For the most part, people have been amiable and frequently intrigued at the discovery that there are two of us. Only once have I felt any acrimony. When I contacted one book dealer to inquire about the possibility of stocking some of my titles, he lit up like a Christmas tree upon hearing the name, but brushed me aside gruffly when he discovered that I was not *the* Hal Roth. "If you ever see him," he tossed the dismissing comment, "you can tell *him* to stop by."

Finally I decided it was time for the two Hal Roths to get together. I wrote a letter, suggesting that we meet for lunch. It was answered by a neighbor, who informed me that Hal and Margaret were on the Mediterranean, retracing the journey depicted in Homer's *Odyssey*, but would return across the Atlantic after the end of the hurricane season.

A few months passed, and one day the mail included a letter: "I'd be delighted to have lunch with you. Give me a call, and we can set a date."

I was wrapping up a book and involved in the madness of preparing for its publication, and I let some months slip by without responding. "Call Hal Roth" was transferred repeatedly from one list of things to do to another.

And then one morning I knew I could no longer put it off. The mail that day contained a check from a book distributor, made out to Hal Roth and to my address. The problem was that I had no unpaid bills with the company, and the book titles and address on the enclosed invoice were his.

"This is the other Hal Roth," I announced when he answered my telephone call, and then explained about the check and suggested several solutions.

Hal and Margaret Roth Aboard Whisper

"You could always spend it," came his amused reply.

Instead, we met and lingered over lunch, and I found myself listening with fascination to a recounting of his Mediterranean travels, retracing the journeys of Odysseus, an adventure which occupied Hal's and Margaret's lives for nearly three years, and about which Hal was then writing a book.

Odysseus, known to many by his anglicized name, Ulysses, was king of Ithaca and a hero of the Trojan War in Greek legend. He became the central figure in Homer's *Odyssey*, the epic poem portraying his perilous wanderings—encounters with Cyclops, Poseidon's son; the Lotus-eaters; the cannibal Laestrygones; the enchantress Circe; the ghosts in the Land of Shades; the Sirens; Scylla, the sea monster; Charybdis, the voracious whirlpool; the Cattle of the Sun—and his years with the sea-nymph Calypso on her lonely island.

"I had the idea of retracing Odysseus's travels for some time," Hal explained, "but my editor didn't think I could do it. He said it would take a certain maturity of experience and viewpoint. He was probably right, but that was twenty years ago, and I've had some time to think about it."

To begin their odyssey, Hal and Margaret sailed from St. Michaels to Cape Charles at the mouth of Chesapeake Bay, then to the Azores, on to Gibraltar, and across the Mediterranean to Turkey—nearly halfway around the world.

"In this project," Hal said, "I discovered that the *Iliad* and the *Odyssey* are books that everyone thinks they've read, but in truth they've really never read them. I soon realized that I had to tell the story all over in very brief, simplified terms. And you can't get into the *Odyssey* until you know about the *Iliad*, so in the beginning I had to retell the *Iliad*, which I did in one thousand, nine hundred and forty-three words."

(The book, *We Followed Odysseus*, was published in 1999.)

The other Hal Roth was born in Cleveland, Ohio, the son of an orchestra leader. "But I haven't been back for a long time," he explained. "I went off to the U. S. Army Air Force when I was seventeen."

"You must have needed special permission to enlist at seventeen," I said.

"Oh no," Hal replied. "In World War Two they were glad to take seventeen-year-olds. 'Young men of seventeen,'" he repeated a recruiting slogan as though he was reading from a poster, "'you too can win your wings of silver. See your U. S. Army Air Force recruiter.'"

Hal was trained as a crew chief and engineer, "But I was essentially a mechanic," he said. "I did a lot of flying in B-25s, and later I got checked out as a panel engineer in B-29s."

Recalled to uniform during the Korean War, Hal again flew in B-25s, this time on mock missions against our own F-86 Saber Jets, testing America's west-coast defenses. "Most of the time they couldn't find us," he recalled. "It's a good thing the Russians didn't know how lousy our air defenses were."

"With the wars and what-not," Hal reminisced, "it took me a long time to get through college." He graduated from the University of California at Berkeley in 1952 with a degree in journalism and ambitions to break into newspaper work. "But," he explained, "newspapers were beginning to feel the iron fist of television and were folding up like yesterday's edition. I couldn't find a job, so I started freelancing, and I've been doing it all this time."

By 1956 Hal was writing for *Collier's* magazine. "That was a big thing," he remembers. "They raised hell with me: 'You're writing for *Collier's* now,' they said, 'so we expect you to stay at the best hotels and eat in the best restaurants, and your expense account should reflect this.' Unfortunately the magazine went out of business the following year."

In the early years Hal also wrote for *Argosy, Blue Book, Coronet,* the Sunday supplements: *This Week Magazine, American Weekly,* and others, and was a photographer for *Saturday Evening Post.* Today he writes for several sailing publications.

Hal's wife, Margaret, who is English, was born in Bombay, India, where her father was an engineer for that city's port.

She and Hal met in San Francisco.

The couple began sailing with friends in California in 1962. "We liked it," Hal said, "but we didn't really know how to do it, so twice we charted a yacht with a captain, once in Greece and once in the West Indies. We learned a lot about it." He paused for a second: "Well, we learned something about it."

They bought the first *Whisper* in 1966 (the second is presently moored at St. Michaels), and in 1967 sailed through the southern and western Pacific to Japan, returning to California across the northern Pacific, past the Aleutian Islands, Alaska, and Canada. The adventure found an audience in the book, *Two on a Big Ocean*, and in a successful documentary film.

Then, after their voyage around Cape Horn, the couple moved to the East Coast and made a trip around the world from 1981 to 1985. In 1986-'87 and again in 1990-'91, Hal completed two additional circumnavigations, east-about in the southern ocean, each time alone in a fifty-foot yacht.

Few couples have lived a closer life—the cabin on *Whisper* served as Hal's and Margaret's home for nearly thirty years, often on the high seas. Hal's dedication in *Always A Distant Anchorage* sums up their relationship succinctly: "To Margaret—the best mate a man ever had."

"You'll be seventy-two on your next birthday," I reminded him; "when do you plan to stop crossing oceans in small boats?"

"I don't know," he replied. "I have a lot of book ideas; I take them one at a time."

"And what are your plans when you finish with Odysseus?"

"I wrote a book some years ago called *After 50,000 Miles*, a technical book about sailing. It was quite successful, so I'm going to do a new one called *After 200,000 Miles*. It will be along the same lines."

Hal has also written a book about mountaineering, *Pathway in the Sky*. I asked him if he has done a lot of climbing.

"A fair amount," he replied, "but now I'm lucky to get up the stairs."

I don't know about the other Hal Roth's agility on stairways and mountains these days, but I'm betting that many miles of ocean waves still lie in his future. And as for this Hal Roth, he really is lucky to get up the stairs.

The Other Hal Roth at a Book Signing in Easton, Maryland

Postscript

Since writing this article for *Tidewater Times*, I have received additional checks intended for the other Hal Roth, have been invited to do a radio interview about one of his books, fielded several telephone calls, including one from Western Canada, and I have continued to disappoint his fans at book signings and other events.

But I have also experienced something new. While visiting the California State Library Haiku Archives in 1999, I discovered his *Pathway in the Sky* cataloged with my work, and at a boat show in Atlantic City recently, he reports that he was looked over quizzically by a woman struggling to find me in his features.

As this book goes to press, Hal and Margaret are preparing to leave for Newfoundland. "We've never been there, and I don't know what we'll find," Hal told me, "so we're just going up and see what happens."

What you should expect to happen is another outstanding book of sailing adventure.

∞

My father used to tell this story. It was in the 1890s or maybe a little after that. It was in the days when preachers engaged in repartee with the congregation during the sermon.

The regular preacher was away, so they brought in a very young fellow who was aspiring to be a minister. He preached about Jesus feeding the multitudes by bringing in many wagon loads of food. After the service, somebody took him aside and told him how it really happened.

So next Sunday the boy preached on the same theme, except this time Jesus fed the multitudes with two fish and three loaves. And as he was telling it, he called out to a man in the congregation: "Captain Billy, could you do what the good Lord done?"

"Well," Captain Billy said after thinking on it for a minute, "I could if I had what you brought with you last week."

∞

Here We Go Again

I warned you once that you just can't believe everything you read, and it's good advice to revisit that thought from time to time.

It was initially with disbelief, then anger, and finally with considerable sadness that I read a recent article in *The Sun*, Baltimore's daily newspaper and a vehicle which I had previously thought to be above the temptation of involvement in the dark dealings of regional politics.

The piece by Frank D. Roylance, a member of *The Sun* staff, was titled "Maryland's First Baltimore" and included a color photograph of a man identified as "An archaeologist employed by R. Christopher Goodwin & Associates of Frederick," working, the caption claimed, "at the Old Baltimore excavation site."

I "knew," of course, that they had to be talking about Vienna on the Nanticoke River, which, as numerous documents have revealed, was originally intended to carry the glory of the Baltimore name down through the annals of our history. Such was clearly the wish of Lord Baltimore himself.

In my excitement to learn the details of the archaeological investigation, I failed to ponder why I had not encountered conversation about such a project on my daily visits to Vienna. A scientific dig should have been a compelling topic for discussion in the post office lobby.

The first clue that I was about to suffer intellectual trauma came with the dateline: "ABERDEEN." Then my excitement was completely shattered by the first paragraph: "In the 1680s the frontiersmen and tobacco merchants of the northern Chesapeake Bay gathered to trade and socialize at a tiny tobacco port on the Bush River." Roylance went on to claim that this heretofore neglected center was called "Baltimore Town."

"Oh boy," I caught myself muttering aloud, "Here we go again!"

We see it everywhere today: people plotting to rewrite history—revisionists attempting to convince our youth that the Holocaust never happened, that Native Americans were not the first nomads to populate North America, that *all* of our presidents have been philanderers, etc., etc. Our own navy has even come to deny that Maryland's beloved *Constellation* was built in Baltimore and carried the young nation's colors with honor in the War of 1812.

The headline on page 7A in *The Sun*, where the outrage concluded, was even larger than the banner on page 1 and shouted, "Archaeologists Unearth Old Baltimore."

"We have very few windows on the 17th century," the digger Polglase is quoted as saying, while comparing the Bush River site's importance to that of London Town [on the South River in Anne Arundel County] and to parts of Annapolis and St. Mary's City.

Delmarveans will immediately recognize that all of these locations are on the western shore. No mention is made of the numerous and sometimes earlier sites on the Eastern Shore. Indeed, the first English settlement in Maryland was on Kent Island.

Here on Delmarva, where the news media strives against the pressures of politics to retain its tenets of honor and truth, the Aberdeen frontier village and tobacco port has been presented to the public in a far more truthful and less spectacular manner. In Easton's *Star Democrat*, for example, the headline announcing the Harford County activity stated: "Archaeologists dig up settlement." It is factual, non-political, and to the point, as headlines should be.

This new campaign on the part of the Baltimore-Annapolis power brokers, as subtle as it may appear to the citizens of Maryland who live west of the Chesapeake Bay, is just another attempt to distort our history and enviously suppress the Eastern Shore. By now you have probably taken notice of the fact that the western shore has not yet gained proper-noun status as has the Eastern Shore, but it is also the result of a recent election in which the offices of governor and comptroller have been filled for another four years.

"What's the connection?" you ask.

The connection is that the winning candidates for the aforementioned offices failed to gather enough votes in the nine counties of the Eastern Shore to warrant the expense of having had their names printed on the ballot. Once more they were "elected" to office through all-too-familiar tactics employed perennially by those who would keep the Eastern Shore poor so they can enjoy cheap vacations and seafood—vote early, vote often, and bring all your friends and relatives from the graveyard.

It's payback time again, and the "Old Baltimore" article is only the tip of the iceberg drifting across Chesapeake Bay. When you hear the story Grandpa Hurley shared while we were sampling a few swigs of his cider fermentings last week, you will better understand just how insidious these people can be.

Grandpa Hurley, one of Delmarva's living legends, resides quietly in the shack that was once Senator T. Coleman duPont's duck-hunting camp in the great Dorchester County salt marshes. Aside from a few liberties taken in the telling of fishing and hunting anecdotes—for which God surely excuses all mankind—I have never known the old timer to stretch the truth so much as the diameter of a strand of two-pound-test monofilament.

Grandpa Hurley's shack is situated just inside the Clam Snout election district, and the rocker on his front porch commands an unobstructed view of the only land thoroughfare into town. If you want to know who's coming and going in Clam Snout, there's no better well of information than Grandpa.

Some time before the Clam Snout deadline for candidate registration—which by charter occurs on the day before election—Grandpa took notice of a strange chauffeur-driven car coming and going at unusual hours. The fellow in the back seat was dressed like a chicken-necker, and Grandpa says he's seen Willie Don in so many Rick Kollenger cartoons that he would know him anywhere.

Celebrities, of course, come and go on the Eastern Shore, and Grandpa, not being an obsessively curious man, did not spend a great deal of time pondering why a big-ticket western shore politician would be wearing his tire treads down on the road to Clam Snout, but he mentioned it anyway when he went to town for a haircut.

Chris Wiley, sixth-generation proprietor of Wiley's Barber Shop, Fish and Produce Market, Family Restaurant, Bar, and Fur Dealership, which sits right next to the bridge at the end of Main Street, is, like Grandpa Hurley, in a position to know who's coming and going. He hadn't seen Willie Don coming at all, but he had noticed Rufus Zert going a lot. Putting two and two together, Chris and Grandpa figured out that Rufus and Willie Don had been consorting somewhere in the marsh between Grandpa's shack and Clam Snout.

Clam Snout, you will need to understand if you are to grasp the subtleties of this unfolding tale, has a two-member town board, and one of those posts is filled by Jimmy Lungrell. Jimmy was elected "ad infinatum" after he ran the Virginia oyster pirates out of Clam Bay back in the 1870s. Jimmy died in 1901. Rufus Zert once filled the other post.

Rufus, you also need to be informed, is a "come here," his great, great-granddaddy having moved down the bay during the War for Southern Independence. There was some talk at the time about the elder Zert keeping a picture of Lincoln in his bedroom, and so there has always been a considerable amount of suspicion about Rufus' politics.

Rufus was elected to the second post on the Clam Snout Town Board in 1968, it having been unoccupied since Jimmy Lungrell's grandson refused to be reseated upon his return from the battlefields of France in 1918.

Needless to say, Rufus's election came as quite a shock to the citizens of Clam Snout. What he had done was to drop off a write-in ballot at the unattended poling place in Captain John's crab shack, which also serves as Town Hall. It was the only ballot cast in 1968.

In 1972, Rufus ran unopposed for reelection and lost to Becky Zebo. He was the picture of confidence that morning as he drove his wife and two daughters to the poling place. The ballot count was thirty-two for Becky and one for Rufus. The citizens of Clam Snout had learned the lesson of write-in ballots well.

Becky Zebo grew up behind the counter in Zebo's Country Store, so everybody in town knew her since she was in diapers. To make her candidacy even more attractive to voters, she then lived in Pine Neck on the other side of Clam Bay and hardly ever visited anymore.

Becky's administration of municipal affairs was so admired by townsfolk that they reseated her in 1976 and in every election thereafter, even though she married a man from California and moved to San Diego in 1975. The Clam Snout Town Board, understand, has no prescribed duties and exists solely for the thus far unthinkable possibility that it will someday be needed.

After 1968 the ballot box was moved to Wiley's Barber Shop, Fish and Produce Market, Family Restaurant, Bar, and Fur Dealership and has never again been left unattended. Since their 1968 lapse of vigilance, the townsfolk have accepted their right to vote as nothing short of a sacred responsibility.

Needless to say, Rufus Zert has been steaming and scheming ever since his involuntary retirement from politics. Clam Snouters had hoped Rufus would move back up the bay after it occurred to him in 1992 that his wife and daughters must have cast their ballots for Becky Zebo, and he subsequently divorced Mrs. Zert.

But Rufus has stuck tight, ever wakeful for an opportunity to return to office.

At this point I need to reverse the prop and let you have a look up another gut for a minute, so you can see how Willie Don got involved.

Just before Willie Don made his move to grab Maryland's purse strings in 1998, he happened to be headed for Ocean City with his chauffeur one weekend and stopped in Oysterback looking for a cheap bushel of crabs. Captain Hardee Swann had the only jimmies in town, and Willie Don found him holding court on his usual bench in Omar Hinton's store.

Since Captain Hardee had to go down to the wharf to get the crabs, Willie Don decided to take a drive around town.

This was right after the Crapo Papers had gone on display in Doreen Redmond's Curl Up 'N' Dye Salon de Beaute, and Willie Don, being a naturally nosy person, decided to check them out. He had read only as far as Lord Baltimore's plan for a metropolis on the banks of the Nanticoke River, when Captain Hardy showed up with the crabs.

For the rest of the drive to the beach, Willie Don plotted how he might profit from what was sure to be a major boom in real estate once the new town sprang up, but first, he figured, he needed to find a local to act as his operative—no easy task when you've offended everybody between the Bay Bridge and Ocean City by referring to the region as the "outhouse" of the state.

And so the stage was set: Willie Don searching for a front man and Rufus desperate for some political clout to return him to office. They met in a singles' chat room on the internet and set out to bend the course of history.

After a few powwows in the marsh, Rufus agreed to seek out some cheap land along the Nanticoke, which he would later sign over to Willie Don, while the Baltimore power player offered to buy the vote for Rufus and throw in a state-funded replacement of the Clam Snout drawbridge, which had stuck in the open position so many times in recent years that Chris Wiley was getting ready to order a new sign to read: "Wiley's Barber Shop, Fish and Produce Market, Family Restaurant, Bar, Fur Dealership, and Ferry."

But after all their plotting, the whole sordid business collapsed when Zeke Elliott, in an act unprecedented in Maryland history, moved his family from the Eastern Shore to the western shore and let the cat out of the bag about how the Nanticoke deal had fallen through sometime back in the 1600s.

The rest is history: Annapolis, of course, cut funding for the bridge as soon as the election was over, but Clam Snouters are prospering under another Jimmy Lungrell and Becky Zebo administration, and everybody is invited to the dedication next week of the new sign for Chris Wiley's Barber Shop, Fish and Produce Market, Family Restaurant, Bar, Fur Dealership, and Ferry.

∞

When we moved down here, we had never talked to a soul about anything. The day we moved in, we were straightening up, and someone knocked on the door. A lady from the neighborhood invited us to have dinner, which was a really nice gesture. While we were eating, she began to tell us where we had moved from, how many children we had, how many grandchildren we had, where I'm retired from. . . . Now we had never talked to a soul down here till we talked to this woman. It still befuddles me how she got all that information.

∞

Blackbeard
on Chesapeake Bay?

Federalsburg, Maryland, which sprawls around the navigable head of historic Marshyhope Creek, is not a place where one would expect to encounter tales of pirate gold, but it was in the center of this Caroline County community where June Truitt told me about her grandfather's quest for Blackbeard's treasure. June's grandparents lived in the woods near Tanyard Branch, and her grandfather swore that Blackbeard, whom he referred to as "Bluebeard," had buried a chest in the swamp nearby.

"My grandfather was dead at this point," June explained, "but Grandmother used to say that on a certain moon—when the moon was full—grandfather would take a divining rod and go out to look for this treasure. He would get a sounding, Grandmother said, and that rod would just tremble. And as soon as the rod trembled, a cloud would go over the moon, and a thunderstorm would come up. It was the pirate wanting to chase him away from the gold because Charlie was right on it. Grandmother believed it too," June said. "Don't you just love it?"

The late Lee Harper, who lived half a dozen miles downstream from Federalsburg, was less skeptical of the buccaneer's connection to the Marshyhope, historically known as the Northwest Branch of the Nanticoke River.

"Blackbeard wintered in Puckum Creek one year," Lee informed me, "right across from my aunt's place. She found that information in some book. She's deceased now, but it was right across from her house. Blackbeard sailed up here and stayed all one winter, and my ancestor, John Harper, jumped ship. That's where we got started here on the Eastern Shore."

There are other references in folklore to Blackbeard visiting the Nanticoke and Wicomico Rivers—even the Transquaking—and burying chests of stolen wealth.

Arthur Little, who lives at Cox's Corner near Tyaskin, told me there is an island on the other side of the Wicomico River, not far off Whitehaven, where people claim Blackbeard buried treasure. "I used to work with mosquito control and dig ditches for draining marshes," Art said, "and we always hoped we'd dig it up. But we never did," he chuckled.

Around Tilghman Island there is still vague talk among watermen about Blackbeard visiting the mouth of the Choptank River and leaving behind a sunken chest, and while Hulbert Footner was gathering material for his delightful *Rivers of the Eastern Shore* (1944), he spoke with a man identified only as "an old riverman." While driving from Cambridge into South Dorchester one summer day, he told Footner about the treasure in Jake's Hole, a ninety-foot-deep depression near the mouth of Watts Creek.

According to the old waterman, Blackbeard dropped an oaken chest encircled with copper bands into Jake's Hole and left behind a school of man-eating red herring to protect it. Many knew of the treasure, but none could outwit its guardians until an Englishman named Longbow built a home on the river. One day Longbow took his visiting cousin, Prince Fakir, on a tour of the river. While they were passing Jake's Hole, Longbow was attempting to teach his guest to sing "Yankee Doodle." This amused the red herring so much that they laughed themselves to death, thus opening the way to the treasure.

But alas, Blackbeard had left another curse as well. It

was easy enough to snag the chest with grappling hooks, but whenever it was brought to the surface, the ropes burned through with an awful stink of sulfur, and the booty sank back into the depths. And there it remains if you want to try for it.

But before you begin to weigh your gold, there is an additional problem you will encounter. The ADC's Chartbook of Chesapeake Bay lists neither Watt's Creek nor Jake's Hole in its index; nor could I find any mention of them in the map-books for Dorchester or Talbot Counties.

Footner's informant also offered details of how Blackbeard came to his untimely end. "That was off Sharp's Island," he told his captive audience. "Blackbeard was lying in wait under the island at the edge of Dick's Hole for a richly laden East Indianman that was expected down from Baltimore. He was so intent upon it he failed to notice the tops'l schooner *Julia Harlow* lying inside the hook. Young Joshua Covey was her master. Covey was able to creep up on Blackbeard in a yawl boat and to board him before he was discovered. Covey cut off Blackbeard's head with one mighty sweep of his saber."

But pirates the stature of Blackbeard do not die easily. Before disappearing, the buccaneer tossed a copper plate, upon which he had recorded the location of all his treasure caches, into Dick's Hole and, headless, jumped overboard and swam three laps around the boat.

Tilghman Island appears to be the northern limit for Blackbeard stories, but one's imagination is stirred when entering the Chester River. After passing Kent Island Narrows, and just beyond Winchester Creek, the river bank is designated on charts as Bluebeard's Bluff; then, on the other side of Walsey Creek, before Coursey Point and Queenstown, one encounters Blackbeard's Bluff. The references seem obvious, but I have yet to be informed of the tales which area residents must once have told.

Blackbeard is also reputed to have deposited heavily laden

chests in the vicinity of Smith and Tangier Islands, where folklore is rife with stories of treasure.

One legend, which has several versions on Tangier and a-long the Pocomoke River, centers on a large family and a restless spirit unable to achieve peace until it gives away its ill-gotten fortune. In all accounts the husband is detained while returning home late one night by whisperings, which emanate from an old house or from the darkness of the forest. The man, who lives in poverty with his wife and children, is intrigued by an offer of riches, but becomes so fearful that appeals to follow or to rendezvous at a later time are rejected in panic. The yarn has a happy ending, however, as one of the children, a retarded boy, thereafter returns home with gold coins whenever he goes out in the woods to play. When questioned, the child replies that a man with a long, blue beard gives him the coins. In each of these tales the pirate is referred to as "Bluebeard."

Not that he was in any danger of being forgotten, Blackbeard recently made the headlines again when what is believed to have once been his flagship, *Queen Anne's Revenge*, was discovered buried on a sandbar in twenty feet of water, two miles off the coast of North Carolina.

And who, actually, was Blackbeard, this individual among thousands of pirates who sailed and plundered during the seventeenth and eighteenth centuries, who has come to stand at the top of his profession as a household name?

Although most books claim that Blackbeard's name was Edward Teach, many primary documents show that he went by the name of Thatch, a nickname for the devil, and the surname Drummond appears on at least one early source. 1680 or thereabouts is believed to be the year of his birth.

Bristol and London in England are suggested by some references as his origin. Others say he was from Jamaica, and even Philadelphia and Accomack, Virginia, have been touted as his home. It is believed that he sailed out of Jamaica with the crew of a privateer during Queen Anne's War [War of the

Spanish Succession—1702 to 1713].

Evidence indicates that Blackbeard began his piratical career under the command of Benjamin Hornigold when he was appointed to captain a captured sloop in 1716. The earliest public mention of his name was on pages of the *Boston News-Letter* in October, 1717.

In the eastern Caribbean, in November, 1717, after raiding the Atlantic Coast as far north as Delaware Bay, Hornigold and Teach seized *Concorde*, a twenty-six-gun French slaver, richly laden with gold, silver, and jewels. Teach requested the vessel as a reward for his services. Hornigold consented and soon retired from piracy, accepting a pardon from the British Crown. Increasing *Concorde*'s firepower to upwards of forty guns, its new captain renamed her *Queen Anne's Revenge*.

Soon afterward Teach encountered Stede Bonnet and invited the "gentleman pirate" with his ten-gun sloop, *Revenge*, to join in the search for booty. During the winter of 1717-1718, with the incompetent Bonnet tightly under his control, Teach cruised the Caribbean, taking prizes and adding two smaller vessels to his fleet.

When it turned northward in the spring of 1718, the command consisted of four vessels and perhaps as many as seven hundred pirates. A blockade, usually considered to be Blackbeard's most notorious achievement, was mounted against Charleston, South Carolina, in late May. The eight or nine vessels and crews taken during the harbor's closure were exchanged at the end of a week—minus their valuables—for a chest of medicine, and the pirates continued northward along the coast.

A week later *Queen Anne's Revenge* was lost on a sandbar off Beaufort, North Carolina, deliberately run aground on the pretext of cleaning the hull. Here she lay forgotten until marine archaeologists recently discovered the wreck and began excavation. The real reason for destroying the flagship was to break up the company of pirates and allow Blackbeard and a small group of hand-picked friends to escape with the valuables.

Teach suggested that Bonnet take his men to accept a pardon offered by the provincial governor, promising to hold their share of the booty until they returned.

Bonnet would never see Blackbeard again.

Marooning additional men on a deserted sandbar, Blackbeard sailed to Bath, where he received a pardon from Charles Eden, North Carolina's Governor and a man long suspected of collaborating with pirates for a share of their wealth.

But neither Blackbeard nor Bonnet were content to retire, and both soon returned to the taking of prizes. The hapless Bonnet and his crew were captured near present-day Wilmington, North Carolina, in October, 1718, and taken to Charleston, where they were tried and all but four hanged.

Concerned about coastal raids and lacking confidence of any assistance from North Carolina, Virginia's Governor, Alexander Spottswood, sent two Royal Navy sloops, *Jane* and *Ranger*, into his neighbor's waters under the command of First Lieutenant Robert Maynard with orders to take Blackbeard. The story of the ensuing battle differs slightly from teller to teller. This is one version:

The two vessels arrived off the Outer Banks on November 21 and, after entering shoally Ocracoke Inlet, discovered their quarry at anchor in a sheltered cove. Blackbeard, having been warned of the expedition against him, met his guests with cannon fire. As the day progressed into twilight, Maynard found the channel too dangerous to continue. Blackbeard and his men spent the night drinking and waiting for Maynard to play his hand.

In the pre-dawn glow off Ocracoke Island, Maynard ran up the Union Jack on *Jane,* and Blackbeard responded by raising his personal black ensign bearing a horned skull. There was so little wind that the boats had to maneuver with oars. The captains hailed each other from their respective bridges, and Maynard was later quoted as saying, "At our first salutation, he [Blackbeard] drank damnation to me and my men, who he stil'd cowardly puppies, saying he would neither give nor take quarter."

As Maynard approached his adversary, the pirates raked his sloops with cannon fire. Maynard, having no cannon, responded with muskets and ordered his seamen below deck.

Apparently taken in by the ruse, Blackbeard drew alongside *Jane* and boarded with ten of his cutthroats, only to be immediately engaged by a superior force. After a violent and bloody free-for-all, the pirates were defeated, and Blackbeard lay dead, struck by five pistol balls and bleeding from more than twenty saber cuts. Twenty-nine of Maynard's sixty-four men were either killed or wounded.

Maynard severed the head of his antagonist and hung the bloody trophy from Jane's bowsprit. Blackbeard's body was cast overboard, and legend claims—remember the tale of the old Dorchester riverman—that the headless body defiantly circled the boat three times before it sank.

As a warning to any who might consider taking up a life of piracy, Spottswood displayed Blackbeard's skull on a pole at the mouth of Hampton River. It was later retrieved, some declare, by "brethren of the coast" and fashioned by a silversmith into a cup, bearing on its rim the inscription "Deth to Spotswoode."

Two skulls, each reputed to be Blackbeard's, have been displayed by the Mariners' Museum in Newport News, Virginia.

A tall man with a powerful physique, Teach earned his sobriquet by sporting a long, bushy beard done up in numerous braids and tied with multicolored ribbons. When preparing for an assault, he slung a bandoleer with three braces of pistols—all six primed and cocked—over his crimson coat and supplemented them with an assortment of swords and daggers. To enhance his already fierce appearance, Teach tied pencil-thin matches—slow-burning fuses normally used to ignite cannon charges—beneath his hat. As he approached an intended prize, the matches were lit and lent a ghastly, smoldering appearance to his face.

Blackbeard from an Engraving by B. Cole in the Mariner's Museum

Blackbeard was an early master at the art of psychological warfare. Standing tall and menacingly on the bridge and shouting that he was brother to the devil and that resistance would result in a swift and certain trip to hell was usually enough to gain capitulation. Captives were customarily robbed and released unharmed.

Take another look at the time frame. Edward Teach received his initial command from Benjamin Hornigold in 1716, was first mentioned by the media as a pirate in October, 1717, and a short thirteen months later his severed head was swinging from *Jane*'s bowsprit. How many historical figures have achieved such an enormous and enduring reputation in such a short period of time?

But to all you seekers of Blackbeard's treasure on the islands and along the tributaries of Chesapeake Bay—sorry folks, but there is not a single documented scrap of evidence to indicate that he ever came closer than to sail past Cape Charles and Cape Henry at the mouth of the estuary.

∞

Things was a little bad back then in the depression times. You just didn't have everything. The Model A Ford was a big car in those days. There was a store over to Hawkeye, and that fella had a hole cut in the floor with a piece of rat wire over it. When it was ninety degrees outside, the air comin' up in that hole in the floor was about eighty. You'd go in there, and you wanted to know if he had any cold drinks. He would say, "I got some air cooled." He had four or five cases settin' on top of each other, right in a pile over that hole, and he called them "air cooled." Well, that sounded good back then. You didn't have no ice. We didn't have electric till later in the forties.

∞

The Ghost
of Cannon Hall

In the tranquil community of Woodland, Delaware, where the Nanticoke River runs its tidal course within a forested border fringed by tuckahoe and wild rice, a substantially framed manor house, which is listed in the National Register of Historic Places, dominates the waterfront. One writer has portrayed it as vigilant for a return of the sleekly trimmed schooners and pungys which docked in the mansion's shadow when Woodland was known as Cannon's Port and engaged in commerce with trade centers as distant as Europe and Africa.

Jacob Cannon (1780-1843), the son of Jacob Cannon (d. 1780), built Cannon Hall around 1820 in anticipation of his marriage, but his fiancee changed her mind about the wedding, and he never lived there.

In the 1930s, while investigating the legend of Patty Cannon, F. Arthur Laskowski visited Cannon Hall and had this to say about the imposing edifice: "At Cannon's Ferry is Cannon Hall, the large dwelling in which lived Isaac and Jacob Cannon, brothers of Jesse [Patty's husband]. In the kitchen is an enormous fireplace with a large brick platform. In front of this a man was murdered, and a short time ago the blood stains could be easily distinguished."

Most of Laskowski's research consisted of listening to the oral traditions and folklore of area residents. He was careless about recording his sources and apparently made no attempt to verify the information he reported as fact. There is no record of either Jacob or Isaac Cannon ever having resided in Cannon Hall, and Jesse was a distant cousin, not their brother, but Laskowski's description of the kitchen fireplace is accurate.

In 1994 Cannon Hall was purchased by A. V. and Marilyn Griffies and their son, Jeff.

"We were looking for an old historic house to work on," Mrs. Griffies told me, "and we just love it."

I asked her if she had heard Laskowski's account of the murder and if there were any stains in front of the fireplace. She knew nothing of either but surprised me with her own story:

"I had never seen ghosts and never thought about them one way or the other—whether they were real or not. It was about a year after we had moved here—at Christmas time. I was in the kitchen cooking, and the TV was on. I was mixing something and heard a noise in the attic above the kitchen. That's my son's office. I turned the TV off, and it sounded like someone was walking around up there, but I knew my son and husband were both at work. At first I thought maybe Jeff had come home, but I looked out, and his truck wasn't there. This house has noises all the time, especially in the wind, but it wasn't anything like that—it was somebody walking around. I didn't think about ghosts; I thought somebody was up there. I got so scared I called the police. I thought somebody would come down the stairs any minute. I stood by the kitchen door ready to run out.

"The police came, and there wasn't anything.

"Then a few weeks or a month later I saw her in a room in the attic. It was just her head! She had medium-length blond hair, and she looked to me to be in her thirties, maybe late thirties. I can still see her now. It was so clear and so fascinating; I just sat there and could not believe it. She was across the room and was floating towards me, and she kept getting closer and closer. I couldn't take my eyes off her. I wasn't scared. I knew what it was, but it wasn't any-

Jeff and Marilyn Griffies with Sammy

thing scary. It was totally fascinating."

The vision eventually disappeared.

"We don't know who she is, but we think it might be Luraney's daughter [Luraney Boling was the sister of Isaac and Jacob Cannon]. She lived here after her mother died. Sometimes I hate to tell people that I've seen her. Some laugh, but I know what I saw.

"We have felt her presence, and my son has felt her presence. Sometimes when you walk into a room, you can feel she's there. She's been in my bedroom, she's been in the bathroom upstairs, and she's been in my son's bedroom. It's hard to explain. When you walk into the room, you just know somebody is there. It's been months now since she's been around, and I can't wait till she comes again."

I asked a woman who investigates the paranormal for her evaluation of Mrs. Griffies' experience.

"There are different types of hauntings," she told me. "Some are actual—where the consciousness of the spirit is still present. Others are residual—where the consciousness is not within the spirit. In the residual hauntings the same actions play over and over like an old movie, and the spirit shows no signs of interacting with people. There are quite a few stories about folks that witnessed partial spirit apparitions, and usually they include the head."

A short distance below Woodland Ferry a small tributary enters the Nanticoke from the northwest. The road to Galestown crosses this branch on Maggie's Bridge. In the woods nearby, a hidden, mostly desecrated graveyard accommodates several generations of resting Bloxoms. Maggie is believed to be one of them.

Sometime in the late nineteenth century is the closest anyone can now come to dating the tragedy of Maggie Bloxom. Few details of the accident are known. Maggie was thrown from her horse-drawn carriage and decapitated. The girl's misfortune, an area resident insists, is a fact, but Maggie Bloxom has also become a legend. Some say that when the moon is full, Maggie can be seen riding her horse, eternally in search of her head. "Stand on the bridge," I was told, "and call her name out just right, and she will come out of the woods." Others claim she carries her head in her arms.

It seemed logical to me that a connection could be made between the story of Maggie Bloxom and the head described by Mrs. Griffies, but her son Jeff says the family makes no tie between the two events. "I know my mother uses the term 'head' when she tells the story," Jeff explained, "but the vision was of a face rather than a bodiless head."

In the dining room of Cannon Hall, some months after our initial conversation, I asked Mrs. Griffies if there had been any other encounters with the ghost.

"No," she answered quickly, then, responding in the same breath to a non-verbal communication she had picked up from Jeff, asked, "There has?"

"I've been meaning to tell you," Jeff began, "but we've been so busy this morning. Last night, when I went up to the attic to put a box away, the light flickered. As I started down the stairs, I felt as though someone was watching me. I turned around and went back up, hoping to see her. I didn't see anything, so I started down the stairs again, and then I felt a hand on my shoulder. I got a real sharp twinge, like someone had a grip on me. But I wasn't scared," he quickly added.

"It didn't scare us when I saw her," Marilyn Griffies interrupted. "We can't wait to see something again; we want to."

"Some people," Jeff continued, "see ghosts wherever they go. We've never seen anything before. But come," he said, "I'm going to take you outside for a minute."

We exited the exquisitely furnished old manor into the bright sunshine of a spring afternoon. In the yard adjoining the ferry house property my host stopped and pointed to an old tree.

"You know the story about Jacob Cannon being shot and killed on the ferry wharf. He had an argument with Owen O'Day over a bee hive in a tree. This tree right here—there's a bee hive in it. We're not sure whose property it's on. People have said, 'You should cut that down before it falls down.' The state [Delaware owns the ferry house property] says it should be cut down. From what I can tell, it's on our property. So here we are, living in Cannon Hall and having a dispute over cutting down a tree with a bee hive in it. A little dejàvu, wouldn't you say?"

Even a brief visit with the Griffies will leave a visitor with the firm impression that Sammy, the Griffies' terrier, is the de facto owner of Cannon Hall. I have heard that some dogs seem especially sensitive to a spiritual presence and wondered if Sammy has shown any awareness or apprehension around the house.

"No," Jeff responded, "Sammy has been very comfortable here."

Marilee Bradley owned Cannon Hall for thirty years and resided in it for twenty, living alone there after her husband's death and her son's marriage.

"I never had the same experience as Mrs. Griffies," she said. "I just wondered if I wasn't perceptive enough. But I did have something happen before we moved in. I was painting the dining room woodwork on an autumn afternoon with my ladder close to the entrance to the basement. I heard steady, heavy footsteps come up the cellar steps. I'm not a person who gets frightened. I can see myself now, just standing there with my paint brush tossed in the air, waiting for the door to open. I was looking at it, but nothing happened. So I got down off my ladder, opened the cellar door, and there wasn't anything there—just cold air. That was the only thing that ever happened to me."

In theory, a ghost is the remnant of what was once a human being and is capable of exhibiting all the mental attributes of the living: emotions, emotional needs, morals, calculation, ego, personality—everything, in fact, that makes up the human psyche. Some believe that ghosts are spirits which have been unable to achieve rest, most notably when death is accompanied by great physical or mental trauma.

Woodland has certainly known its share of untimely death. In addition to the tragedies of Jacob Cannon, Maggie Bloxom, and a variety of other violent accidents and murders during its early history, local tradition holds that smallpox came to this remote river settlement in the early years of the twentieth century. It is believed that a sailor on a ship from Philadelphia was the carrier. Armed guards, it is said, were stationed at entrances to the town to prevent traffic either in or out.

"My grandfather," a lifelong resident told me, "was living on the other side of the river at the time and traveled by shad barge between his farm and Seaford, paddling upriver on the flood tide and returning on the ebb. He stayed close to the other side of the river, hoping he wouldn't catch it."

Perhaps twenty residents died, a significant number of casualties for such a small village. Will Massey, the ferry operator at that time, is said to have lost two or three of his family. Bodies were wrapped in sheets and buried behind the church in unmarked graves.

"My grandfather wouldn't have turned a shovel full of dirt there for all the money in Seaford," my informant said. "He claimed it [smallpox] never dies."

In recent years Woodland residents have attempted to locate and mark the graves, but the State of Delaware seems to have no record of the epidemic or the burials.

Each year on the second Saturday of September, the tranquillity of this charming little river town is temporarily shattered when thousands of visitors descend to enjoy and participate in the Woodland Festival. Cannon Hall is one of the many attractions, and for this special occasion the Griffies graciously welcome callers to their home and try to answer the many questions posed about its history. During the last festival a man approached Mr. Griffies after touring the second floor and matter-of-factly remarked, "You've got a ghost in here, haven't you?"

Cannon Hall

∞

Well, I don't smoke. One time the doctor told my husband, "Smoke cigarettes instead of eatin' all the time." One Sunday night I decided I'd try it, and so help me this, I'd rather have a chocolate bar.

∞

The "Come Here"

There have always been two primary classes of people on the Eastern Shore of Maryland, those who were born here and those who weren't.

"On Tilghman," an old waterman told me, "if your gran'-daddy weren't born here, an' you ain't growed up crab linin' an' arster drudgin', or have somethin' to do with it, your a furriner."

Everybody knows what a foreigner is, of course—a person born in or coming from another country—but to many a Tilghman Islander it's anyone who was born west of the Chesapeake Bay, south of the Choptank River, or north and East of Route 50, and many a soul within those boundaries is suspect as well.

Lower down on the peninsula one is more likely to encounter the term "come here." To most people who were not born on the Eastern Shore, these words embody a feeling of friendliness—an invitation to approach. But in this instance we are not talking about a verb, nor any familiarity; what we have here is a two-word noun. A "come here" is one whose birth occurred elsewhere—a "furriner," if you will—and the only action involved may be an unspoken suggestion to go back to where you came from. For some who trace their Eastern-Shore lineage back to the seventeenth century, a "come here" is anyone who doesn't. Logically, individuals who are not "come heres" are known as "from heres."

The tradition, ironically enough, may predate those who

take the greatest pride in being "from heres." You have probably heard stories about how, when Captain John Smith explored the Eastern Shore in 1608, he encountered Native Americans calling from the river banks, some climbing into trees so as to project their voices all the farther. Unschooled in the sentiments of these early Eastern Shoremen, Smith apparently made the error of assuming their whoops to be friendly invitations to "come here," and was therefore astonished to be met with volleys of arrows when he approached the shore. The Indians, rather than seeking Smith's companionship, were probably hurling an already time-honored, derogatory label at the unwelcome Englishmen.

Each town or area seems to have its own standards for qualifying a "come here." For those who live in isolated communities and embrace the political far right, boundaries may be tight. I know a "from here" on Elliott Island who considers a "come here" to be anyone from the other side of the bridge at the edge of town. If you live on Elliott, of course, you have to drive a considerable distance on the other side of the bridge before you encounter any life beside marsh critters. On the other hand, the ultra liberal among native Eastern Shoremen will generally accept those born anywhere on the peninsula south of the Chesapeake and Delaware Canal as "from heres," while among middle-of-the-roaders there is a wide disparity of agreement. The worst place you can come here from, naturally, is the western shore, and please note that you must never, ever, capitalize that nether world.

I'm not from here; I'm a "come here." I take no pride in that fact, but there's absolutely nothing I can do about it. It's like the old man once told me—he was pushing ninety at the time. He said, "My parents moved here when I was less than two weeks old, and I ain't never lived nowhere else in my life, but it don't matter, nobody ain't never gonna let me forget I'm a "come here." When I die, and the preacher's a-standin' over my vault, the first thing outen his mouth, he's gonna say, 'Well now, old John weren't from here.'"

When I was growing up in Pennsylvania's Lehigh Valley, among the highlights of each year were visits from a family friend who had moved to Sharptown, Maryland, before World War II. At least twice a year he would show up with a new collection of spellbinding tales about the Nanticoke River and the great Chesapeake Bay marshes.

After completing military service during the period of the Korean War and later earning a college degree, it seemed only the evolution of a kind fate that two ladies appeared on my college campus one day and offered me a teaching position in Anne Arundel County, Maryland. Close enough, I figured, and never sought another interview.

A few short weeks after taking up residency on that nether shore, I was in Dorchester County, brushing up a duck blind at the Forks of the Nanticoke. At that time I considered it one of the greatest fortunes of my life that the Bay Bridge had opened to traffic a few years earlier.

The years rolled along, and I continued to work across the bay, sneaking over the bridge whenever the opportunity presented itself to hunt, fish, boat, hike, camp, birdwatch —anything to get outside and away from that other shore. I recall one blustery New Year's morning when I drove to the Elliott Island marshes before sunrise, with fewer cars on the road between Anne Arundel and Dorchester than I have ever experienced again, just to watch the sunrise on Langrall's Island.

Then, late one Saturday evening in the spring of 1972, the telephone rang and changed the course of my life. "This man died," the caller announced," and his little farm is for sale. I think it might be just what you're looking for." I was in Dorchester County the following morning, walking over a run-down, twenty-six acre mixture of woods and wet, sandy fields with the man who had called. An auction was scheduled for the following Saturday on the bank steps in Vienna.

April 20 dawned wet and windy—the dogwood storms, as

old shoremen call them. After a brief, wet powwow in front of the bank, proceedings were moved down the street under the overhang of Granville Hurst's service station. Barely sheltered from the driving sheets of spring rain, with the attorney for the estate making jokes and small talk while the auctioneer kept pleading for an end to it, I bought the property.

Since that day the details of the sale have been related to me so many times and by so many people that an unknowing eavesdropper could easily be convinced the entire male population between Easton and Salisbury, as well as representatives from surrounding states, must have been present. I remember the crowd as being something less than two dozen.

As we completed the preliminary papers for the sale in the dry interior of "Flat's" station, I asked the attorney if he had any objections to also representing my end of the proceedings—conducting a property search and registering the deed for me. He had none.

Several weeks later, sitting at the attorney's kitchen table to conclude business with the executor of the estate, I asked for the first time how much I owed for legal services. "Well," Ted McAllister said with a smile, "I'm just a poor country lawyer. Is twenty-five dollars too much?"

While my education in the rhythm of Eastern Shore living had begun many years earlier, its pace now quickened.

I had always been inquisitive—the kid who needed to know the history and workings of all he encountered. Names of things were especially important.

In front of the old house on my new property stood a very large and impressive tree. Its bark and shape informed me instantly that it belonged to the maple family, but until the new leaves unfolded, I did not know how to identify the species. I asked my friend who had tipped me about the auction.

"It's a yard maple," he said casually.

"Well," I proceeded carefully, trying hard not to behave

like a "come here," "I was wondering which kind of a yard maple it is—if it's a red yard maple, a silver yard maple, a sugar yard maple, or what."

"All I know is yard maple," he replied with a shrug. "It's what everybody calls 'em."

"How many kinds of maples do you have around here?" I inquired.

My friend furrowed his brow in thought for a moment, then, raising a finger for each species, he slowly enumerated: "There's the yard maple, the woods maple, and the swamp maple."

I was both amused and delighted by the answer. The "book" name for my tree was totally irrelevant to this man, and why should it have been otherwise. Suddenly it seemed much less significant to me. What became important was to know and understand my new neighbors.

Nevertheless, when another friendly "from here" caught me working in the front yard the next weekend and stopped his pickup to chat for a few minutes, I casually threw out the question again.

"That's one of them yard maples," he replied without a moment's hesitation.

Not fifteen minutes later another vehicle ventured down the dusty road, and its driver got out and introduced himself as the nephew of the former owner. Standing beneath the maple, which was now leafing out nicely, he carefully looked it over—fondly I thought—and said, "I had many a good time right here in this yard. I would come to visit Uncle Tommy on Sundays, and we would sit right here under this tree and listen to the ball game." He talked on for a few minutes, extolling his relationship with Uncle Tommy while constantly searching the broad crown of the maple. Finally, bending his head back as far as human anatomy permits, he gave it one more searching examination and said, "You know, you ought to cut it down."

"Cut it down—why?" I stammered in my astonishment.

"It's got to have snakes in it," he replied, making a final suspicious survey overhead.

As Uncle Tommy's nephew shuffled off, I called after him: "Do you happen to know what kind of a tree this is?"

He flung the reply over a shoulder as he entered his car: "It's a yard maple."

Although by this time I was quite satisfied and proud to be the custodian of a "yard maple," I did pose the question to one additional "from here," whom I encountered holding court on the well polished bench in a nearby country store. After this gentleman and I had resolved several major world crises and evaluated the current political hopefuls, I asked him what he did to earn his living.

"Timber," he said with some pride. "Been cuttin' timber most of my life."

Ah ha! I thought, here is a man who knows his trees.

"Have you noticed that big tree in my front yard?" I asked.

He had.

"What kind of a tree is that?"

He hesitated not a second: "It's one of them yard maples," he said. "She ain't much for timber, but they're nice for shade."

I tell you this story because I consider the experience to have been a major stepping stone in my education toward a life less objective and stressful on the Eastern Shore.

Eventually I retired from an administrative position with the Anne Arundel County Board of Education and cast off all residential ties with that other shore. Now, like any "from here," I have grown to dread the few times each year that I am required to cross the bridge.

Because of a compassionate tolerance displayed by the many friends I have made on the Eastern Shore, I have learned to live with the fact of being a "come here," but something new has crept into the lower-shore vocabulary, and several weeks ago I was called a "chicken necker!"

"Chicken neckers," like "come heres," are outsiders—generically, those week-end crabbers who share the widespread belief that chicken necks were created by God as the world's most noble crab bait. The late Captain Lester Lee from Queen Anne's County is usually given credit for popularizing the title around Kent Island. While I'm not sure if Captain Lester actually coined the term, William Warner certainly made him and the label famous in the prize-winning book about watermen, crabs, and the Chesapeake Bay—*Beautiful Swimmers*.

As evidence of the growing popularity of this moniker, there was recently a "chicken-necker.com" internet site, maintained as a support group for fellow "chicken neckers" by a self-declared and proud "chicken necker" named Bill Evans. The site is closed now, but in the tradition of Jeff Foxworthy and his widely popular "You-might-be-a-redneck-if. . . " monologue, Bill had built a repository of "chicken necker" lines. Consider that you just might be a "chicken necker" if you think the Bay Bridge was a sign of progress (boy, did that one ever hit home), or if you cross it for anything but a wedding or a funeral. Doing your Christmas shopping in St. Michaels is certainly a reliable clue to such a heritage, and demonstrating any love whatsoever for William Donald Schaefer puts you automatically and firmly in the chicken-necker camp.

All of this makes for good humor, of course, but being called a "chicken necker" just doesn't rest lightly on my ego. As I explained at the beginning, I first learned to love the Eastern Shore and its people many years ago as a boy living north of the Mason Dixon Line. While the land and its inhabitants have only become more and more dear to me with each unfolding decade, I accept the reality that in the final judgment none of that matters a particle. Stamped on my citizenship papers, right behind my name, are the words "come here," and when that preacher is standing over me in the box—well, you know the rest. But please don't call me a "chicken necker."

∞

A Legacy in Clay

Pottery is one of man's oldest crafts, and archeologists are often able to use the distinctive shards they find to identify human cultures and date ancient dwelling sites.

Before the arrival of European colonists in the early part of the seventeenth century, Delmarva Indians made pottery vessels to serve as reservoirs for water and for cooking. Women collected the clay they found exposed on the surface of the ground and along waterways. This raw material was kneaded and beaten with stones, boards, or simply with bare hands. Foreign material was removed, and the refined clay was tempered with water and with particles of pulverized mineral or shell to give it substance and strength.

Although the potter's wheel had been invented nearly five thousand years earlier, when John Smith explored the Chesapeake Bay in 1608, he found Native Americans using a simple coil technique to construct their vessels. First, they rolled lumps of clay into long, cord-like pieces. This "rope" was then laid out on a flat surface and wound in a spiral, each layer pressed on top of the preceding one as the sides of the container grew. Fingers pinched the coils together, wooden paddles patted the utensil into shape, and flat stones were utilized to burnish the surface until it was smooth. Nanticoke pots had a rounded base.

The earliest vessels were simply set out to dry in the sun, but as the use of fire increased, man learned that baking the clay would turn it as hard as stone.

In school, kids sooner or later are handed a piece of clay. Most play with it for an hour or two and fashion the pliable lump into some sort of curious shape. If the object ever reaches home, parents will display it for a brief period of time, relatives and guests will compliment its creator, and soon afterward it will disappear forever.

David Warfield's first pot, hand built in an art class in 1976, still sits in his living room along with a sampling of other efforts which have emerged from his kilns over the ensuing years.

"In high school," says Warfield, "I touched a piece of clay, and I never stopped. I took an art class. I could draw halfway decent—nothing great—but I just loved the clay. I don't know why. I grabbed that first piece of clay, and something happened. I was hooked."

After graduation, Warfield continued to live with his parents, and his bedroom became his studio. Remembering one pot from those days, he chuckled. "I made it in my bedroom and had no place to fire it. It was close to three feet tall, so I put it in a truck and got a friend to sit in the back and hold it. It was greenware and very fragile. We drove for five or six miles through Baltimore City to the Maryland Institute of Art. I went in, and the guy said, 'Yeah, I'll fire it for you.' He didn't even charge me.

"After school I went to work," Warfield explained, "to buy clay."

His first job was at a crematory. "I actually fired a pot in the crematory one time," he recalls. "I made this pot and stuck it in with a dead guy to fire it, but it blew up. I put a lot of hours into it. It was a nice, detailed face—a sculpture—and it blew up. I was upset."

"Why would it do that?" I wondered.

"It's kind of technical—thermal expansion," Warfield tried to explain. "The crematory didn't get as hot as my gas kiln does, but the problem was that it heated up too quickly."

The Vienna potter shook his head. "That was a strange

job," he said. "I worked there for eleven months and then got a job at a hospital in Baltimore. I was the 'gofer' for their maintenance department, but I ran all over the place for all the departments. That's where I learned about working for the other guy. [It is very clear that he wasn't pleased.] After that I drove a tractor trailer for a scrap metal company."

"And what about pottery during that time in your life?" I wanted to know.

"I was making pots and a little bit of sculpture just to satisfy myself," Warfield replied. Then I went to work for a fellow who supplied kilns, potter's wheels, all kinds of tools, and custom-made clay. I was his 'back.' I mixed a ton of clay a day, and that's when I discovered that some people did this full time.

"I was making clay for this guy and that guy, and I wondered, 'What are they doing with all this stuff?' I asked one fellow, and he said, 'It's my job. I've got to make a lot of pots if I want to make any money.' I said, 'That's all you do?' I just never thought it could be a full-time job.

"So then I figured, 'Hey, I can do that; I can make pots.' That was it. I got started in a shed I built at my parent's house, and I did some shows. Now people ask *me*, 'Is this all you do?'"

Although he once was able to, as he puts it, "pop a few grand at a show on a weekend," Warfield seldom attends shows these days. His wholesale business takes up nearly all of his time and energy.

The majority of his output is distributed in four states: Maryland, Delaware, Pennsylvania, and Virginia, with a scattering in Florida, the Carolinas, and Kentucky. He is looking at the possibility of acquiring outlets in New York and on the Outer Banks of North Carolina. Annapolis, Newark in Delaware, Alexandria in Virginia, and the District of Columbia are his major markets, and there may be a web site in his future.

While we talked, Warfield applied handles to stoneware soup tureens. He painted an almost liquid clay on each end of measured clay strips, applied these precisely to the pleasingly curved sides of the bowls, and molded and smoothed the joints until the individual parts became a single elegant work of art.

David Warfield at his Potter's Wheel

"You've got to twist the handles just right," he commented, "so they blend into the pot."

Warfield is modest about his skill as a potter. "I've never made a perfect pot," he says. "No one can fully master clay."

Then, as if he immediately had second thoughts about his view of mastery, Warfield said, "Marilyn Levine—she's the best at what she does. She has a piece called 'Bob's Jacket.' There is a rack on the wall with four hooks, and this leather jacket hangs on one of the hooks. It's worn and has wrinkles in it. If you saw it, you'd think it was real, but it's all solid clay. She also did a pair of steel-toed boots with the leather busted off and the steel showing through. The laces are untied and laid out on the floor. She can do a piece like that and get $10,000. I put handles on soup tureens and make coffee mugs to pay the bills."

Warfield's principal output is stoneware: a variety of pots, pitchers, crocks, cups, bowls, creamers, mugs, tureens, three styles of oil lamps, several electric lamps, soap dispensers, vases, etc., etc., etc. "To put food on the table and fix this old house," he explains. He would really prefer to spend more of his time and talent doing crystal glazes and creating raku.

"Crystal glaze is very involved and difficult, and that's why I want to do it—just for the challenge," he says. "Firing must be very precise. The result is similar to ice crystals on a window in the wintertime. Sometimes you get large crystals and sometimes small ones.

"Raku is fun. I don't want to sound like a weirdo, but I like to fire. With raku, you're in there; you're almost in the fire. You pop that door open, and it's eighteen to nineteen hundred degrees, and your legs are on fire, and you grab that red-hot pot—it's just neat. Of course it can really tick you off when they're not turning out and you're losing them left and right. There's no control, but it's exciting when you get a good one."

Raku is a type of pottery developed in the Far East hundreds of years ago. Japanese raku ware is unusually soft for a ceramic and is fired at low temperatures, making it possible to decorate the pieces with wax-like glazes, including a unique shade of subtle salmon. No two pieces of raku are ever alike.

"The raku I make should technically be called American raku," Warfield explained. "In the early '60s, Paul Soldner started it all, and he probably discovered the technique by dropping a red-hot pot on the ground. When it rolled, it burned the grass, and that made the cracks black." Warfield admits he is guessing but adds, "A lot of things come from accidents."

Soldner is credited with originating what potters call "post firing reduction." A piece is taken directly from the kiln and smothered in sawdust or, theoretically, in any combustible material. "Anything that burns will work," says Warfield. "You could wrap the pot in your shirt."

The blanketing material smolders in contact with the pot and emits carbon, and the carbon penetrates and stains the exposed raw clay areas. There are special formulas for mixing the clay to achieve the best results.

Warfield purchases fifty-pound bags of pulverized clay and mixes it himself. There are many kinds of clay and many potential additives to achieve the great variety of results which are possible. Potters use recipes not unlike chefs. "That pot," says Warfield, pointing to one of his tureens, "has four different clays as well as silica and feldspar in the mixture."

His largest kiln, a gas-fired furnace which he constructed himself, has a stacking space three feet deep, five feet high, and two feet wide, with another foot of combustion area on each side where the flames enter. "I can stack a couple hundred pots in there," he says. When fired at night, the entire cubicle glows like a vision from Dante's Inferno.

While Warfield earns his living as an artist, he is considered by friends to be a jack-of-all-trades. He is currently winding down the ground-to-attic renovation of a hundred-year-old Victorian house in Vienna, which he purchased in 1996—a residence which had been occupied only by termites since 1968.

Warfield Unloading the Kiln

Like so many others, Warfield was attracted to Delmarva by its water and slower pace of living. "I like the water," he said. "I like going out on a boat, crabbing and fishing, or just taking a ride."

"I was looking for an old church or schoolhouse or barn to renovate because I didn't have much money. It was the day after Christmas in '95, and I was driving around. I had a map and a highlighter. I was marking the roads that I went down. I was looking everywhere.

"When I first saw this house, it was dark—about seven o'-clock at night and cold and windy. There was a 'For Sale' sign on the front lawn. I looked at it, and I said, 'That's my house.'

"I went right up to the gas station and called the agent. She told me, 'I just put a contract on it.' I said, 'I want that house!' It was a wreck, but I could see a lot of neat things about it. The other guy couldn't come up with the money, and I bought it in February, '96."

His first projects were to hook up the plumbing and con-struct an addition to the garage, which serves as his studio. Remodeling of the house is a work in progress.

If the proficiencies I have already mentioned are not e-nough to impress you, add mechanic to the list of Warfield's achievements. It is a practical talent for someone who hits the road each day in a 1982 van and cruises the rivers of the Eastern Shore in a 1962 inboard-outboard runabout.

"And how did an artist become accomplished in such di-verse professions?" I wanted to know.

"Just by doing it," Warfield responded casually, as though construction and mechanical skills are no more complex than changing a light bulb or reading the oil stick in your Chevy. "It comes from watching my father; he's a genius. A buddy of mine always called me 'son of genius.' My father is an electrician by trade, but he can do anything."

On days when he sits down at the potter's wheel, Warfield throws fifty to seventy-five pieces. He has no idea how many he fires in the span of a year. The Nanticoke Indians who grubbed for clay along the river near Emperor's Landing, now Vienna, would be amazed to watch him at his potter's wheel. It was no less fascinating for me.

Warfield Poses with an Unfired Face Jug

∞

If a horse's tail is full of knots in the morning, you know it has been ridden by a witch the previous night.

∞

Witchcraft
in the Free State

The belief in witchcraft has existed from ancient times in both primitive and literate societies. In the Code of Hammurabi—Babylonian laws (c. 2000 B. C.) which were rooted in earlier Sumarian law and based on the familiar principal of "an eye for an eye, a tooth for a tooth"—we find some of the earliest written penalties for witchcraft: "If a man has put a spell upon a man and has not justified himself, he that wove the spell upon him shall be put to death."

While the Bible reflects a similar attitude: "Thou shalt not suffer a witch to live," the early Christian church was more inclined to punish adjudged witches by excommunicating or imprisoning them. It was not until the thirteenth century, with changes to Canon Law espoused by Gregory IX, that sorcery came to be rewarded by burning at the stake. Joan of Arc is probably the most famous victim of this enlightenment.

Pope John XXII (1326) helped to clarify specifics by ordaining that penalties should be imposed on all "who ally themselves with death and make a pact with hell, who sacrifice to the demons, make or have images, rings, mirrors, phials or other analogous objects intended to serve as bonds to hold the demons, who ask questions of the demons, obtain answers to them, and have recourse to the demons to satisfy their depraved desires."

Suspicion on the part of almost anyone was cause to investigate an individual as a practitioner of witchcraft, with death-bed testimony given particular weight. Other considerations included:

—testimony of a fellow witch or magician, or of a wizard offering to show the witch's face in a glass;

—testimony of two witnesses of "good and honest report";

—if death or "some mischief" followed a cursing, quarrel, or threats;

—if a suspect was the offspring, servant, friend, neighbor, or companion of a convicted witch;

—if the suspect was found to have "the devil's mark"—a mark with no evident natural cause—or if the devil offered to give testimony under oath. (I have no explanation of how the latter might have been accomplished);

—if the suspect was inconsistent or contradictory in answering questions;

—if the suspect called upon the devil or desired his help;

—if the suspect "entertained a familiar spirit and had conference with it in the likeness of some visible creature";

—if witnesses affirmed under oath that the suspect accomplished any action which "necessarily infers a covenant made, as, that he hath used enchantments, divined things before they came to pass, raised tempests, or caused the form of a dead man to appear."

A free and voluntary confession of the crime by the suspect after examination was primary evidence for a guilty verdict, and many accused witches filed guilty pleas. No matter that such acknowledgments generally succeeded sessions on the rack or the application of thumb screws, all confessions were termed "voluntary."

Disposition of witches by both church and secular society also included stoning, decapitation, and drowning. By the time America got into the act, hanging appears to have been the remedy of choice.

In the superstitious minds of crewmen aboard the *Charity of London*, bound for St. Mary's City, Maryland, in 1654 and daily growing more leaky, there could be only one reason for their misfortune—witchcraft! While no specifics have been preserved, it was the result of "her own deportment and discourse" that suspicion fell upon a woman named Mary Lee, and demands followed that she be tried according to the customs of the day. The ship's master, John Bosworth, decided, instead, to put her ashore in Bermuda. When cross winds prevented the desired landfall and storms placed the *Charity* in further danger, Mary was apprehended and searched by the crew. Finding the "signal or mark of a witch" upon her, the seamen tied the unfortunate woman to the ship's capstan.

On the following morning "the signal was shrunk into her body for the most part," and Mary "confessed" to being a witch. The crew then demanded she be put to death. When Captain Bosworth exhibited reluctance and retreated to his cabin under their vehement demands, the sailors satisfied their fears of Mary Lee by hanging her. This incident, recorded in the *Maryland Archives* through the testimony of Henry Corbin, a merchant of twenty-five years, and Francis Darby, a gentleman of thirty-nine, is the first Maryland reference to the killing of a witch.

Maryland's passion with witchcraft never approached that of New England's, where the hysteria in Salem, Massachusetts, peaked with the execution of nineteen individuals in 1692, while a hundred other citizens were imprisoned, including ministers and children, and another two hundred stood accused.

Someone once remarked, only half jokingly, that the difference between Maryland and Massachusetts may have lain in the truth of an observation made by Richard Baxter, a prominent English Puritan minister, who said, "Where will the Devil show most Malice, but where he is hated. . . ." Perhaps the devil was on better terms with the citizens of Maryland.

John Washington, the great grandfather of George Washington, became a complainant in Maryland courts in 1658 against Edward Prescott for the execution of Elizabeth Richardson, accused as a witch aboard Prescott's ship, the *Sarah Artch*, bound for the colony. When it was determined that Richardson, owner of the ship on which the act took place, was not the ship's master, and when Washington failed to appear in court because he refused to postpone his son's baptism, the accused was acquitted.

Many believe today that witchcraft indictments were only brought against women, and that the deck was always stacked against the accused. Neither assumption is correct.

When accusations of witchcraft against Elizabeth Bennett were presented to the grand jury of Philip Calvert's Provincial Court at its October, 1665, term, she was cleared of the charges by proclamation.

The first guilty verdict in the province was entered against John Cowman, convicted under the Statute of James I, in 1674, for "witchcraft, conjuration, sorcery or enchantment upon the body of Elizabeth Goodale" and sentenced to be hanged. In spite of the fact that they referred to Cowman as a "wretched and miserable object," deputies and delegates of the Lower House of the Maryland General Assembly petitioned Charles Calvert, Lieutenant General and Chief Judge of the Provincial Court, for clemency, and the Upper House, on February 17th, 1674, granted a reprieve. To make a lasting impression on Cowman, the Sheriff of St. Mary's County marched him to the gallows, placed the rope around his neck, and there informed him of his good fortune. The felon was then ordered to remain in St. Mary's City and be employed in services to the governor and council as they saw fit, for as long as they saw fit. We are probably safe in assuming that Cowman stopped messing around with the body of Elizabeth Goodale.

While an appalling number of individuals were executed throughout Europe, it speaks well of Maryland law and administration that so few formal charges were brought against suspected witches, and only one woman, Rebecca Fowler, ever paid the supreme penalty.

Rebecca was the widow of John Fowler, a Calvert County planter, and was indicted as follows: ". . . Rebecca Fowler the last day of August in the year of our Lord 1685 and at divers other days and times as well . . . having not the fear of God before her eyes, but being led by the instigation of the Divell [sic] certain evil and diabolical arts called witchcrafts, inchantments, charmes, and sorceries then wickedly, divelishly and feloniously . . . did use, practice and exercise in upon and against one Francis Sandsbury . . . and several others . . . in his and their bodies were very much the worse, consumed, pined and lamed against the peace and etcetera. . . ."

Rebecca pleaded, "Not guilty."

No details of the proceedings have survived, but on October 2, 1685, twelve jurors declared Rebecca guilty of "witchcraft, charmes and sorceries and etcetera." On October 3 the court sentenced her "to be hanged by the neck until she be dead," and on October 9 the sentence was performed at St. Mary's City. Those were days of timely trial and punishment!

In 1686 Hannah Edwards of Calvert County was charged with similar acts of practicing witchcraft against Ruth Hutchinson and several other persons, but Hannah was declared "not guilty."

By 1712, when the last formal case was heard against an accused witch, the Provincial Court had moved to Annapolis, the new capital of Maryland. In that year, on October 5, Foster Turbutt, Sheriff of Talbot County, presented Virtue Violl for trial, accused as follows: "Virtue Violl of Talbot County, spinster . . . seduced by the devil most wickedly, and diabolically did use, practice and exercise witchcraft, whereby and wherewith she did . . . waste, consume and pine the body of a certain Ellianor Moore [and did] render [her] speechless to the great displeasure of Almighty God and against her majesty's peace. . . ."

Virtue was declared "not guilty."

A great variety of judicial proceedings in colonial times resulted because of the beliefs about witchcraft, but not necessarily in formal indictments against accused witches.

On January 15, 1702, Charles Killburn presented himself to the courts, complaining that he was in a "very languishing condition," which he attributed to witchcraft practiced on him by Katherine Prout. Frequently, Killburn testified, while on his way to recovery, he would meet Prout, and she would abuse and threaten him, specifically stating that she hoped he would never recover his health and would "languish to death."

The court summoned Prout, who proved rebellious. After examination, charges of witchcraft were dismissed, but the justices fined the feisty lady one hundred pounds of tobacco for "misbehavior in her Saucy Language and abusing this Court."

Two months later Killburn brought an action for slander against Prout for calling him a "rogue" and a "foresworn rogue," inferring that he had committed perjury. It was the judgment of the court that Prout pay Killburn six pence, a trifling award, but court costs were assessed for one thousand, one hundred and one pounds of tobacco.

Prout then sued Kate Quillan for slander, the charge being that the latter had called the plaintiff "Dame Ye." The inversion of these words, Prout charged, carried the imputation of witchcraft, since its devotees did or said nothing in natural order. Theft of molasses and "New England Capons" (mackerel) from a cellar in Annapolis was also alleged by Quillan. The plaintiff won an award of three pounds damages, and the name of Elizabeth Prout appears no more in Maryland court records.

Requests to the chancellor for injunctions to restrain an individual from practicing witchcraft or from making false charges of witchcraft were not uncommon. One such petition was made by Joan Michell, who was involved in a variety of litigation over accusations made against her. This 1659 document provides a vivid glimpse into the belief structure and language of the period. It should be noted that punctuation did not become a standard part of written discourse until late in the eighteenth century, and spelling was generally a matter of personal whim.

"Whereas your Poor Petitioner is most shamfully and her good name taken away from her shee doath desire tht shee may bee righted and that shee may bee searched by able woemen whether shee bee such a perrson or no which thos persons say I am and if I bee found to bee such a one I may bee punished by law or els to bee Cleared by Proclamation. . . .

"I desire tht Mr Francis Doughty [a rector of the Church of England] may bring thos Persons to light that haue raysed this schandalous reports of mee for hee sayd that I salluted a woman at Church and her teeth fell a Aking as if shee had bin mad and I desired him to tell mee who had raysed this report of mee and hee woold not and so from one to an other my good name is taken away that I Cannot bee at quiet for them for it is all their delight and table talke how to doe mee a mischief beeing a poore distressed widow . . . for of a sunday as I was going to Church with too of Capt: Fendalls folks Mr Walkers man hurled stones at mee as I was going along and so hid himself again which for any thing that I know his master might set him on to Mischefe mee and hee himself wrongs mee by work. . . ."

Since the seventeenth and eighteenth centuries, America's view of witches has experienced considerable evolution. Today Salem claims a witch population of about three thousand individuals, primarily those belonging to the modern religion known as Wicca. Two thousand more reside in nearby communities. There is a Witches' League for Public Awareness and even an official Witch of Salem, appointed by former governor Dukakis. Many practitioners publicly wear dark robes and black makeup. Some operate shops, selling herbs, oils, and dietary supplements, while others conduct classes.

Although witchcraft continues, occasionally, to make Maryland headlines, it is usually in the form of a human interest profile. There are no official statistics to indicate the number of Wicca practitioners in the Free State.

∞

This old woman down below here, she was a conjure. Everybody knew it. People went to her for to take spells off, or if they needed a charm or things like that. Mostly she done everybody good. Now this was back—maybe just after the World War—the one in 1918. It was the same year the flu killed everybody up around here.

But this one time she took a notion 'bout somethin' this other lady done. That lady lived right across the road—right over to the end of that field—right by the woods there. The house burned down years ago.

This conjure woman—her name was Ruth—she took an auger drill and bored some holes in a great old pine out back. Then she took and carved some pegs to fit in them holes, and she smeared some—well, it was her own manure she smeared on them pegs, and she set 'em in the holes. And every day she went there with a mallet, and she drive them pegs a little bit farther in that pine tree.

This other lady took sick, and every day she had a spell of pains and got worse. Her husband thought it was the flu, but the doctor said he couldn't explain it. It looked like she was gonna die.

Somebody told her husband, "I think there's a spell on her. I know a man," he says, "over by Indian River, and he's a medicine man. Maybe he can help her."

So her husband fetched the man—he was part Indian and part colored—and he said right off that she had a spell on her. He give her some potion to drink, and he asked could he stay in the barn so he might get a notion of what was goin' on.

It wasn't a day, and he caught old Ruth at that tree, and he made her take them pegs out. He told Ruth that two could always play at the same game.

That lady took an upturn right off, and after a week she was near'bout good as new, but nobody ever saw old Ruth a- live again after that. They found her body some later out be- hind her shack, and they buried her across the branch there. It's two roads down, where they cut that timber several year back. Ain't no stone or vault or nothin'. They just put her in the ground.

∞

To keep a witch out of your house you must stop up all the holes, even the keyholes. Then you lay a broom stick across the doorway.

A witch can turn herself into any animal she wants, and she can turn you into a horse or a mule while you're sleeping and ride you all night long.

If a witch sits in a chair where a fork is stuck, she can't get up as long as that fork stays there.

To kill a witch, you must draw a picture of her and shoot it with silver instead of lead. Just where the picture is shot, that's where the witch will be wounded.

∞

Last of
the Shad Men

With the inflection of a man who is talking about something he deeply loves, Jack Knowles said, "I've lived my entire life only a stone's throw from the river."

While his assertion is somewhat rhetorical, the distance between the northwest bank of the Nanticoke and the tidy home in Woodland, which Jack shares with his wife, Carolyn, is no more than a quarter of a mile.

When Knowles was growing up, visits with family and friends were a major part of one's social life.

"In those days," he remarked, "youngsters stayed at home nights. Most of my relatives lived nearby, and I loved to sit and listen to their stories about the Nanticoke.

"Around Christmas they'd start with the shad tales, and I'd hear them all through the winter. By March I was just bustin' to get on that river. Now, by January I am. Listening to those tales is what made me like I am."

While farming was the region's primary occupation, it was the Nanticoke which provided the first income of the year. In January and February residents trapped its cripples and marshes for muskrat and mink; then March brought the spawning migrations of herring and shad.

"Herring was a big industry in the eighteen-hundreds and early nineteen-hundreds," Knowles told me. "People would salt them. They were a mainstay in the wintertime. I've heard my grandfather talk of horses and buggies lining up for half a mile, waiting to buy herring that came out of the haul seine. Haul seining was my grandfather's first job—$1.25 a week. He was born in 1887 and went to work when he was thirteen or fourteen."

Knowles still catches a few herring and cans them. "They took a terrible down cycle like the shad," he said, "but they're coming back. I'll catch a herring the first full moon in January—I like to fish the moons—and we call that a branch herring. It's the kind that goes up in the shallow water to spawn. There used to be thousands of them wallowing up on the shores. You could hear them at night, and it was no trouble to find fifty raccoons along the banks catching them.

"We have two herring runs, and then, about the same time as the shad come in, we get what I call a glut or blood herring. They're smaller, but they're a pretty fish. Blue-back is the proper name. They don't go into the branches. They stay in the river."

Knowles began fishing for shad with his grandfather when he was five, and they fished as a team until Jack was nineteen or twenty. "It was my job to hold the boat so he could twine the shad up," Jack remembers. "That's how I learned to paddle, to hold the boat to the wind or the tide. I paddled until 1953, when I got my first outboard motor—a five-horse Sea King.

"You like to carve a paddle out of ash," Knowles explained, "but ash is hard to find around here. I've had some paddles made of regular old pine. They won't stand a lot, but they're good for paddling.

"When I was a kid, most of the fishing was done at night because the fish could see the cotton and linen nets in the daytime. You could look out and count ten to twenty lanterns on the river anytime. The lantern was placed on a wooden float, and you'd tie that to your net. I'd still like to use a lantern—to me it's better than a flashlight with a battery in it—but it doesn't meet state requirements.

Jack Knowles in his Shad Barge

"They used to tell a tale about an old black gentleman who fished on the river. They said he never used a lantern. Grandpa pulled up one night and asked the man what he was catching. He said, 'Aw, I'm not catchin' nothin'. I just got a cheese box full of nails.' The man was sitting there in the dark, and when Grandpa went over with a lantern, the man had a snapping turtle in his lap, shaking the net off it.

"I remember when there were little cabins up and down the river," Knowles continued to reminisce. "People stocked food in them and went in there to sleep. You liked to catch the slack water, then sleep until the next one."

Only a single cabin has survived, half hidden by brush and trees on Lucas Island, now owned by the State of Delaware.

Nanticoke white shad once averaged about five pounds. Today they run three to four, and they are not plentiful. Knowles keeps only a few each year for himself and friends. Maryland has banned shad fishing in its portion of the river, and Delaware may soon follow suit.

"The first shad will usually appear in a net during the second week of March," Knowles remarked. He quits at the end of the month.

"The height of the white shad run comes around the third week of April, shortly after the rockfish spawning begins. If you've never seen rockfish spawn, it's something to witness. It's unbelievable," Knowles marveled—"thousands of them on top of the water."

Large runs of rock make it impractical to fish for shad.

Knowles claims that gizzard shad are beginning to take over the river—locally they are called mud shad. "My grandfather," he chuckled, "always said that you take the mud shad home and clean him and cook him on an oak board. Then you throw him away and eat the board.

"There's another shad that's shorter, with a blunt nose. He looks like he's run into something. It's an American shad, but everybody calls them 'May shad.'

"When I first started," Knowles continued, "we fished cotton nets. They didn't last over two good weeks of hard fishing."

The procedure for making nets was once a labor of love. Knowles' grandfather would begin the process by boiling spools of cotton line in lard cans.

"Stink!" Knowles winced at the recollection. "You could smell it all over Woodland when Grandpa was cooking lines. Then he'd take the line out and make me drag it all over town. He'd stretch it between poles for about two weeks before making the net. You'd do that to take the kinks out of it. You can take a piece of cotton rope—twisted rope—and hold it together, and it's not worth a nickel, but after you boil it and drag it and stretch it, then it will hold in a perfect loop.

"They used a dye made from walnut and oak to dye the nets, and some would paint the bottom line. The bottom line was called the lead line, but actually it never had lead in it; it would sink without any weight.

"The women spent all winter knitting those nets, and that's hard for me to imagine. They had wooden blocks that were made like wedges—different sized wedges for different sized mesh—and that's what they used as a knitting gage. They would wrap the line around it and tie a knot on the small part of the wedge, and just keep repeating that."

Nets used for shad fishing are gill nets. The openings are large enough to allow an adult to swim partly through; then their gills prevent the fish from retreating.

"I've heard my grandfather talk of catching a hundred and fifty shad on one drift with a cotton net. That's a lot of shad with any net. I wonder what they could have done with nylon. We got our first nylon nets in 1954. We were really uptown fishermen then," Knowles said with a grin.

The term "drift" refers to laying out the net and allowing it to freely move with the tide through a section of the river known as a "reach" or "retch." Fishermen have names for each of these divisions, which are generally based on some prominent physical or geographical feature—Hawk's Nest

Retch, Red House Retch, Flatty Ground Retch, etc.

"When they went to nylon," Knowles told me, "it probably increased the catch three to one, and when they went to monofilament, it increased the catch over nylon three to one. I've fished nylon and monofilament nets at the same time, and I know the catch is three to one."

Maryland has outlawed the use of monofilament nets but Delaware permits them. "I don't think you should be able to use monofilament," Knowles said; "the stuff is lethal."

There is no single cause for the shad decline. Pollution, over fishing, and the damming of tributaries have each contributed. Knowles also blames the offshore trawlers who net the fish as they begin their spawning migration—he calls it the "intercept fishery."

"Will white shad ever come back?" I asked the last of the shad men.

"No! You'll never see it. We're killing them with runoff and ruining their spawning grounds. They're choking the river to death up at Seaford, and nobody's doing anything about it."

The increase in silt has forced Knowles to cut down on the length of his nets—from a hundred and twenty to ninety or a hundred yards.

"We used float nets years ago, but I've gone to shallow nets," he said. "You can't educate boaters to run around the nets, so you let them run over them."

Small floats are still attached every nine feet along the top of the net. Then, along the bottom, directly under each float, a weighted tail is added—sufficient to sink the cork but not enough to allow the net to drag on the bottom.

"You lay the net in the boat lengthwise," Knowles explained, "and 'wrench' it off. I don't know where the term comes from; that's what was passed down to me."

In recent years largemouth bass fishing has become a major sport on the Delaware portion of the Nanticoke River.

"Bass fishermen don't understand what you're doing,"

Knowles said. "They see a net, and they think you're catching everything. I've fished many days and come home with what I had when I started—nothing. The net is geared for specific fish, but the bass fishermen can't seem to realize that. They think that if I've got a net out there, I'm catching all the bass. Some of them curse you and even chunk sinkers at you. In fifty years of fishing I've caught a half dozen bass at the most."

There have always been superstitions which guide the actions of watermen—Knowles refers to them as "rules."

"Most of the time we didn't have a dock, so we pulled the boat up on the shore. The bow always faced the shore, and it was bad luck to turn that boat around before you got out in the main part of the river. And you couldn't talk, and you couldn't keep any noise."

Although Knowles is not a superstitious man, some of the old beliefs may be worth heeding.

"Sometimes when it's calm in the spring, you'll see little patches of sand floating on the river. When you see that, there's no need to go fishing. My grandfather told me that, and it's true," Knowles said.

"My grandfather was also a great believer in the dogwood storms. When the dogwood bloomed, he'd say, 'Get ready; it's gonna get stormy.' It might have nothing to do with shad fishing, but the storms always come when the run is at its height."

Shad barges are exclusively a product of Nanticoke River craftsmen; no other river in the world has known these trim, graceful workboats. There was a time when boat builders in every town along the river produced them, but if you journey from Seaford to Tangier Sound today, you will likely encounter only one. It is docked in Woodland, just above the ferry, and it belongs to Jack Knowles.

"The shad barge is a skiff," Knowles explained, "but barge is the name that's been hung on it around here. The shad barges of the early nineteen-hundreds were long and narrow because they didn't have motors then. The man in the stern paddled, and the guy up front pulled. The man in the front seat used a ten or twelve foot oar."

Jack Knowles' Shad Barge

Although its flat bottom made maneuvering difficult, the historic shad barge could also carry sail and had its mast set into the front seat. Sails were not utilized for fishing but generally were mounted when it was time to haul produce to market. "They'd sail to Seaford with the flood tide," Knowles told me, "and come home on the ebb."

Most shad barges were nineteen to twenty-one feet in length, about three and a half in the middle, and as narrow as ten inches at the stern. They displaced about three inches of water when empty.

"There was always somebody local who built them," Knowles said. "My great grandfather made his own boats."

I wondered who thought of the design—who made the first one.

"I don't know," Knowles answered. "I wish I did." Then he added with a smile, "I always thought that Sharptown made the prettiest ones, even though I don't like to admit it."

Knowles' boat was made by Jake Windsor in Mardela. The sides are constructed of native yellow pine, which Jack, grinning, calls "Eastern Shore mahogany." The bottom is cypress from the Pocomoke swamp, an inch thick and twelve inches wide. Two inches short of twenty-two feet, it measures nearly six across the center. "She'll hold fifteen hundred to two thousand pounds of fish," the owner announced proudly, "but I never have filled it. I had a lot of anticipation when it was built in 1970, but that's when things started going to pot."

Behind Knowles' home stands a metal building, which resembles thousands of garages and farm structures throughout the Delmarva Peninsula, but this one is different; it houses the Days-Gone-By Museum, a collection of artifacts and memorabilia from the heyday of shad fishing and from the Nanticoke River and Woodland area. The gallery is Jack's second passion, but that's another story.

∞

You ever heard of tutter, where in the wintertime a lot of people used to have it? I've had it, but I haven't had it recently. Your skin will crack open, and they call it tutter. Now I don't know—that's the name the old people had, and they'd get sore as the dickens, especially if they're around your nails. If you rub your hands in that cream they rub on cows, it will heal it, but my mother used to say tar soap is better.

∞

Sheriff Andrew
and the Lawyer

The following stories were told to me during several conversations. While editing them to present as smooth a flow as possible, I have essentially retained the language of the narrators. William E. Andrew, in addition to establishing a successful family auction house, served as sheriff of Caroline County from 1938 to 1942 and from 1948 until his death in 1961. He was succeeded by his son Lewis, who continued in that office until 1994. I have honored the request of one of my informants not to name the attorney.

Bill Andrew was sheriff for a long time. He wore plain clothes and drove his personal car, and he never showed a gun—never carried a gun. He had one, but it was always locked up in his glove compartment.

I've seen Sheriff Andrew go into some rough situations. One place was called Chinatown. They'd have a juke box on the corner, and they'd be dancing all over the dirt streets up there in Denton. Bill would walk right through that crowd—no gun nor nothing. He'd tap somebody on the shoulder and say, "Come! You go with me." He'd trail the man right out through that crowd, and nobody would say a word or give him any trouble. He was a magnificent personality.

Sheriffs lived right in the jail at that time. Bill and Mrs.

Andrew raised their family in the jail in Denton, and Mrs. Andrew could contain the bad people almost as good as Bill could. She handled some that the state troopers were afraid of.

You always had a few prisoners you could trust, and they would come out during the day to do some work. They'd keep the coal furnace going and things like that. Bill used to take his old car and go down to the farm with two or three of these trustees, and they'd work on the farm. They'd ride right with him. They never would think of hitting him in the head and taking the car. Before they went back in, Bill would let them play cards. Rook was the game. A lot of times the Andrew boys would be sitting right in the kitchen playing Rook with these fellows.

Most of the prisoners liked Bill. If there was trouble stirring, somebody in the jail would give the others away. There would be a knock on the door where they put pans through to feed the prisoners. A guy inside would say, "I'd like to have an aspirin please," and when they'd come with the aspirin, he'd have a note on a little piece of paper: "Tell Bill not to open the door by himself tonight." They done that a lot of times.

Bill had these two prisoners who were trustees. One was from Delaware, and the other was from Denton. They were big men—forty years old.

Bill got a call one evening. There was somebody from the city they had a warrant for. This fellow would come down to the country on a Saturday night and stay at some place on the weekend. The woman on the phone said the man was there.

So Bill took these two trustees along—him driving. When they got out to this place, Bill said, "Now, they say he's in there. I'm going to the front door, and I want you fellows to get out and go around there to the back door."

So Bill knocks on the door, and he asks for his man.

"Oh," the woman inside says, "we don't think he'll be down this week."

"Well," Bill says, real slow and easy like, "if he shows up, you tell him the sheriff has a warrant for him, and it would make things a lot easier on everybody if he just comes on up."

"Yes," the woman says, "but, like I said, I don't think he'll be down this week."

About that time the back door slams, and then you hear "Wham! Whack! Pow! Bam!"

It's quiet for a minute, and then this voice from out back of the house says, "We got him Bill!"

One time there was a school teacher. I don't know how she ever got acquainted with this guy, but it ended up he was taking over the place, and the lady was scared of the man. Finally she got a warrant for him, and this night she called Sheriff Andrew on the phone and said, "He's sitting out in the barn, and I want to tell you that he's got a loaded shotgun with him."

Bill said, "Well, if you can, tell him I'm coming over to have a talk."

He went down there and got out of the car and hollered, "This is Bill Andrew. I'm going up to the house. Why don't you put your gun away and come on in and talk."

So the man comes in the house and sets down in a big stuffed chair. Bill gets in front of him and starts to read the warrant.

When Bill calls his name, the man stops him. "It's mister," he says.

"OK, mister," Bill says, "now I'm gonna finish reading this, and then we're going to town."

When they got to the jail, the man says, "It's my rights to call a lawyer."

"Sure," Bill says, "you can call a lawyer, but you're still going inside. Who do you want to call?"

The man calls the states attorney.

So they had a conversation, and then he went to jail. They looked his record up, and he had pages and pages of criminal activity—robbery, bad checks, everything.

The county used to have constables to help out. Sheriff

Andrew had a constable named Murphy, but everybody called him "Puss." He would sit and talk to you and slap his head all the time.

Puss went out to pick up a bad guy one day, and he tells the man, "I'm Sheriff Murphy, and I got a warrant for you."

"No," the man says, "don't try to fool me none. You're not the sheriff; Bill Andrew's the sheriff. I ain't goin' nowhere with you."

"OK," Murphy says, "I'm not the high sheriff, but I'm the low sheriff."

"I don't go with no low sheriff," the man says. "If Bill Andrew wants me, you tell him to come get me, and then I'll go up there."

They had a shooting one night down to American Corner. Puss Murphy was at the jail playing checkers, and he got a call from the grocery store. A woman got shot two miles from the store, and a man run all the way down there to call the sheriff. This woman was washing dishes, and somebody shot her through the window. She died, and the undertaker come. They didn't have too many state troopers then, but two of them came over for that. They were talking and talking. They questioned and questioned, and after a while he admitted it. He shot his mother-in-law.

Sheriffs back in those days had to do every kind of thing. They served civil papers and divorce papers and moving papers—everything. They never got credit for all what they done.

At that time there was a lawyer in Caroline County who was a defense attorney, and he could always come up with the answers.

Even after beer had come back legal, there was still a lot of bootleg—moonshining—going on, and this lawyer was defending a bootlegger one time. It was in 1938. Bill Andrew was sheriff and James Deweese Carter was the judge.

This lawyer was always raising the devil about Sheriff Andrew. "I know the sheriff since he was a boy," he'd say, "and he don't know a bit of law, not a bit of law," and carrying on like that.

In this moonshine trial the lawyer kept challenging and challenging one juror after the other, and it came out that they found themselves short. If you ran short of jurors in those days, it was the sheriff's job to go and pick five people off the street and bring them back to choose from to fill up the jury. So the judge adjourns the court and sends Sheriff Andrew out to get some more jurors.

Bill was burning and fuming about all the talk from this lawyer, so he picks up a collection of old maids and preachers and brings them in. When the lawyer sees what the sheriff done, he jumps up and objects. "Your Honor," he yells, "these people would convict Jesus Christ, himself!"

The judge comes right off the bench: "One more remark like that—one more remark—and I'll have you barred from this court forever." That was it. He lost that case, but he won lots of others.

We had no refrigeration before 1948, but we had the smoke house. We could keep pork that was sugar-cured, so there was a lot of hogs. The local farmers—just like they did with wheat thrashing—would help each other out when it come hog-killing time.

Well, when these people butchered hogs, they'd kill them, scald them, scrape the hair off, and hang them up to cool. Then the next day they'd cut them up and make the sausage and stuff.

But this time, when the farmer went down to the barn the next morning, there was this one hog missing. No dogs, no cats, no scratching, no nothing—just gone! After the farmer thinks things over a little, the blame comes to fall on one of the neighbors who helped out. They questioned the man about it, and it wound up that the sheriff charged him with hog stealing.

So the man who was charged with hog stealing went to see this lawyer.

"Now Charlie," the lawyer says, "I gotta know the truth

here. Did you steal that hog?"

"Yes sir," the man says, "I stole the hog. My family was hungry."

"Well," the lawyer says, "let me see here. Do you still have the hog?"

"Yes sir."

"You haven't disposed of any of it?"

"No sir"

"Well, let me see here," the lawyer says. "Tonight, I want you to take that hog and cut it right down the middle, and you bring me exactly half of it."

So that's what the man done.

After that they went to trial, and it happened that this lawyer was a good friend of the judge. The lawyer had this great, orator-type voice, and he has his go-round. He was going on and on—strong. Finally the lawyer ends up his case, and he says, "Judge—Your Honor, you know me to be a man that tells the truth. I will stand here and swear to you on a stack of Bibles that I know for an absolute fact—an absolute fact—that this man has no more of that hog than I do."

The judge bangs down his gavel and says, "Not guilty!"

Another fellow stole a bicycle one time and got arrested, and he went to this same lawyer. They had a little session together, and the lawyer says, "Well, did you steal that bicycle?"

"Yes sir, I did," the man says.

"Well," the lawyer says, "we've got to do some working here to get you off then." He thinks on it for a couple of minutes, and he says, "I'll tell you what you do. When you get up there on that stand, and the prosecuting attorney starts to ask you about the bicycle, you say, 'Wheeeeeeeel!' And every time he asks you about that bicycle, you say, 'Wheeeeeeeel!' Whenever he asks you anything, you just say 'Wheeeeeeeel!' as loud as you can."

So the case comes up before the judge, and the man takes the stand. The prosecuting attorney brings out this bicycle and says to the man, "Have you ever seen this bicycle before?"

The man says, "Wheeeeeeeel!"

"Just answer 'yes' or 'no'; have you ever seen this bicycle before?"

"Wheeeeeeeel!" he says again.

"This bicycle was found in your garage," the prosecuting attorney says. "Can you tell me how it got there?"

"Wheeeeeeeel!"

Getting a little frustrated now, the prosecutor says, "You're under oath, Mr. So-and-so, and you're gonna have to answer my questions."

"Wheeeeeeeel!"

Bang! The judge raps his gavel down on the bench and says, "Get this guy out of here!"

There's an old saying: "When Columbus discovered America, it was full of nuts and berries, and now the berries are almost gone."

∞

Right down this road here—I don't know if you ever been there. Did you know where Levin lived? Well, this was right along in there—just before you get to the marsh—right in that vicinity. I've heard all kinds of stories down there, and it was the greatest mess of stuff—the most gibberish I ever heard.

If you wanted to believe everything you heard, you would believe in ghosts and in witches. You either believe it or you don't believe it, and I don't believe it. I hope my mind never gets so I start believin' in it.

It was a lot of pranks down there, and people would tell you stories, settin' right up there in that barber shop. I know they never thought 'em up 'cause other people sittin' right there would verify it—unless the whole bunch was lyin'.

I'm just gonna give you one example. They was always playin' pranks. Grown men would plan up stuff to scare somebody. Not kids—grown men. They never had no education then. I'm talkin' about people that could talk to you just like I am and didn't know nothin'. Didn't know how to write. Just went out to milk the cows in the mornin' and back in at night is all they knew.

So anyhow, they got after this man always walked up the road in the nighttime—'cause back in the twenties and thirties you had to walk everywhere.

So they took this shotgun shell, and they put bran in it —wheat bran. Some of them people knew how to do all like that. I don't know how many they done. They all planned it up—two or three of 'em—to scare this man.

And this man was walkin' down the road. I don't know, he was up there somewheres, and when they come up to him, they got to arguin' among themselves. They argued, and one fella up with his shotgun and shot that man he was arguin' with. Now this is in the nighttime, and they said when that shell went off, all this bran lit up—it wasn't nothin' but dust to start with. And there was this great big ball of fire. Now you can try that—whether they were tellin' the truth or not. They said it was an awful lookin' sight. That man hollered and took out a-runnin'. They scared him so bad the soles on his shoes actually bursted—him runnin' down that road. Now that's what they always said.

If you had come down the road and seen that, you would say, "Well I seen it," but you wouldn't of knowed that it was planned up. And that's where a lot of that stuff got started.

∞

If you kill a hog on the decrease of the moon, that meat will shrink all up when you cook it.

∞

Ghosts 'R' Us

"I didn't know anything about it," replied Ed Okono-wicz. "I didn't know that adult story tellers existed."

The premier writer of Delmarva ghost tales was respond-ing to my inquiry about how his Spirits Between the Bays Series began.

"And what," I wondered, "does adult storytelling have to do with tracking down ghosts?"

"I wrote an article about a storyteller," Okonowicz ex-plained, "and the woman invited me to a storytelling concert. I picked up a flyer, got interested, took a college course, and started doing adult storytelling—everything from Mother's Day to Halloween, Christmas parties, St. Patrick's Day, birth-days, anniversaries, country inns; and no matter where I went, everybody said, 'Give me a ghost story.' I started buying ghost books for reference, and I said to my wife, 'I bet we could come up with nine or ten ghost stories from this area.' So I put a note in the paper: 'This guy is looking for ghost stories —call him if you have one.' I got twenty-five to thirty calls and came out with the first volume."

The first volume was *Pulling Back the Curtain*, 1994, and for Ed Okonowicz it began a whole new life—at least a whole new chapter in what has already been a very busy and varied career.

Opening the Door was published in the spring of 1995, and *Welcome Inn* debuted in September of the same year. *In the Vestibule* brought thrills and chills to Ed's growing contingent of fans in 1996, followed by *Presence in the Parlor* in 1997, *Crying in the Kitchen*, 1998, and *Up the Back Stairway* and *Horror in the Hallway* in 1999, the latter title selected best short story collection by the Delaware Press Association for that year.

Volume IX of the Spirits Between the Bays Series, *Phantom in the Bedchamber*, will debut about the same time as the book you hold in your hand and will include ghost stories from Gettysburg and a double feature about spirits at Point Lookout State Park and Point Lookout Lighthouse. The beacon at the bottom of Maryland's Western Shore was constructed in 1830, and the site was the location of the nation's largest Civil War prison, which held nearly fifty thousand Confederates. The area is rife with hauntings.

"I enjoyed the trip," Okonowicz told me. "I had never traveled much on the Western Shore. Look at the map and see how far Maryland extends below Washington, D. C., and you can see why Lincoln abused his powers and forced Maryland to remain in the Union, but that's another story for another time.

"You may have observed," Okonowicz offered, "that the titles are leading our faithful readers deeper into our Spirits Between the Bays haunted house. This will continue through Volume XIII, when the reader will be left in the attic or cellar—I haven't decided where exactly."

As a bonus for fans of the supernatural, *Possessed Possessions*, a volume of stories about haunted antiques, furniture, and collectibles, was thrown in for good measure in 1996, succeeded by *Possessed Possessions II* in 1998.

"Wow!" you say, "aren't most writers elated if they can come up with one book every couple of years?" But wait, you haven't heard the whole story.

Okonowicz also produced *Disappearing Delmarva, Portraits of the Peninsula People*, in 1997. This attractive, hardbound coffee table volume boasts seventy biographies with photographs of individuals whose professions are on the endangered list.

Ed Okonowicz in the Welsh Tract Graveyard, Newark, Delaware
Photo by Jack Buxbaum

If you're still not impressed, *FIRED!*, a thriller featuring a cold-blooded murderer who, while being pursued through towns on the Eastern Shore, leaves clues to embarrass the authorities and taunt his victims' families, was released in 1998, followed by the Delaware Press Association's "best novel" choice for 1999—*HALLOWEEN HOUSE.* "This fiction series is not for young readers," warns its author. "Expect murder, mystery, and maybe some unexplained horror themes." His next novel, *HOSTAGE*, will reach bookstore shelves in 2001.

You may wonder if this prolific writer was born with his finger tips attached to a keyboard.

"I was a school teacher for two and a half years after I got out of the army," Okonowicz replies. "I watched 'Mr. Novak' on television and said, 'I want to be Mr. Novak; I'm gonna teach school.' That was the black period of my life. It was hazardous to my health and sanity. 'Mr. Novak' was not the real world, but it was inspiring."

So Edward Okonowicz quit the classroom and became a full-time writer, but you will be astounded again to discover that his job title has been and continues to be editor and writer in the Office of Public Relations at the University of Delaware. Everything I have been telling you about this amazing man, he accomplishes after his 9:00 to 5:00 day job is done.

"I work at the University of Delaware, Okonowicz modestly said, "but this (referring to his books) is what keeps me sane; this is the fun part."

He also writes several pieces for the *Wilmington News Journal* every month, as he has since 1979.

Glancing over an incomplete schedule of Okonowicz's public appearances, I counted nearly seventy commitments in six months. These include story-telling and other speaking engagements, book signings, radio and television appearances —on and on it goes. He gets calls literally from across the country.

"Does the ghost man ever stake out a site," I wanted to

know, "in anticipation of supernatural activity?"

"I'm not one who goes and sits in a house all night and waits," he replied, "but I did spend Halloween Eve in a haunted inn. A radio station asked me to suggest a place, and we stayed overnight. The next morning we were on the air from 5:00 to 9:00 talking about ghosts. The host said, 'We've been here all night and haven't seen a ghost.' I told him, 'We've been here for six hours. I talk to people who have lived in a house for thirty years, and they've had two or three encounters. Be patient!'"

"Of the people you interview," I prodded, "how many actually believe in ghosts?"

Okonowicz was quick to reply: "Generally I would say about seventy to seventy-five percent. They even believe the stuff when I tell them it's not real. I included a story in volume IV about my wife and I going out for our anniversary dinner. We have dinner; then, after we leave the inn, the car breaks down. I return and find it shuttered—the place doesn't exist. A woman said to me, 'You know, I've been looking for that place. Your wife and you had such a wonderful time; I've been hoping to go there. Have you been back lately?' I started to tell her, but she seemed so disappointed that I said, 'You keep looking for it—we pass it every now and then.'

"So you see, some believe even when it isn't supposed to be true—because they want to believe. Maybe it's all the high tech—computers, internet, worldwide web, TV—people want a break. They want to believe there might still be something in the woods. And why not? So I'll say seventy to seventy-five percent honestly believe in ghosts to a degree.

"And then there are the hard core—the ghosts are following them. They talk to the ghosts every day. 'The ghosts are out in the car—do you want to meet them?' One guy called my house and said, 'The ghost is here; it's pushing the walls of the living room in on me. It might be here another twenty minutes. You've got to get over here fast.' That was one of my calls."

"Did you go?"

"No, and he never called back."

"Do children believe in ghosts?" I asked.

"Sure. Think about this: *Goose Bumps*. They come out with several each month. I have kids call me and send me letters. I reply to them through their parents: 'Your son, or daughter, has written to me. Do you want me to talk to them?' I get a large number of kids for book signings and Halloween story-telling, and teachers use the stories in school."

"What about the thirty-somethings?"

"I would say youngsters to about college age, and then from forty up. The area in between—there's either a lack of interest or it's not cool."

"It's been my experience," I told Okonowicz, "that many believe others have seen ghosts, but I rarely encounter anyone who claims to have seen one himself."

"You've hit on it," he said. "I was talking to a fellow recently, and he said, 'I didn't see this, but my mother told me, and my mother wouldn't have said it unless it was true because she was a good, Christian woman.' I've heard that many times."

Most writers consider Ed Okonowicz to be a little crazy, not because he chases ghosts, but because he is one of those rare individuals who enjoys the whole sordid business of making books and getting them into the reader's hands. It's no small accomplishment to put the words on paper, but for writers that's the fun part—editing, designing, typesetting, printing, transporting, storing, promoting, and distributing are considered by most to be nothing short of sheer drudgery. Most writers don't even have a clue as to how it's done. Ed joyously involves himself in all tasks but the printing. At least his hands showed no sign of ink when we talked.

Ed and his spouse *are* Myst and Lace Publishers, or, as I like to call them: Ghosts 'R' Us, and that brings me to Kathleen Okonowicz, whom Ed succinctly sums up as "My wonderful wife."

"As overdone as that statement may seem, I tell you, this is the truth. Without my wife, Kathleen, these books would never come out. Not because I wouldn't finish them, but someone very talented and patient has to put them together. I keep writing, and she keeps designing and laying them out and working with the printer. She is a wonderful business partner and a very good friend, and I respect her judgment. Sometimes it takes a while, but in the end we agree," Ed grins, "and we do it . . . her way."

Don't ask about the cases of books stacked from basement to attic.

In addition to the many hats she wears for Myst and Lace Publishers, Kathleen is a very talented and respected watercolorist. You can see samples of her art on the covers of Spirits Between the Bays.

Okonowicz is a native of Wilmington who now lives in Maryland, half a mile from the Delaware line. "He's a Delawarean," a friend says, "who happens to sleep in Maryland."

Regardless of where he was born or where he lives, Ed Okonowicz has written his way into the hearts of all Delmarvians, "come here's," and "foreigners" who have been fortunate enough to encounter his books.

1999 was a big year for Ed. In addition to his two award-winning books, he was featured on "Ghost Waters," a Learning Channel documentary about the six most haunted sites in America near the water, which aired on Halloween weekend. It was his role as "ghost host" at Fort Delaware, the prison for thirty-three thousand confederate prisoners on Pea Patch Island in Delaware River, which drew the attention of the producers. Ed is entering into his fourth year as co-host of the Friday evening ghost tours at the prison.

As I was driving home from my meeting with this affable gentleman, considering that any profile of him is bound to be out-of-date before the ink is dry, I pondered his parting remarks: "The best thing about all of this is that the search for local ghosts and folklore has taught me a deeper appreciation of the culture and people of the Peninsula, and I've made wonderful friends along the way. Anyone who gets into the business of writing about a region that he loves will be thrilled with every discovery, and he'll never run out of ideas. In fact, you'll go crazy trying to accomplish even a small portion of what you want to do. There is so much out there that we regional writers need to capture—need to preserve before it disappears. The tales, the customs, the old folks' memories are waiting to be shared with us, so we can put it all down and pass it on to our readers. I really believe that's our duty—our responsibility."

∞

There was a man here—he's dead now—and I heard him say one time he had warts on his hands. You don't see too many people with warts nowadays. Him and his father was off somewhere, and he was gettin' his hair cut in the barber shop. The barber noticed his hand, and he said, "Son, what in the world you doin' with all them warts on your hands?"

The boy says, "I don't know. I'd like to get rid of 'em."

The barber said, "You want to get rid of 'em?"

He said, "Yeah."

Now I don't know—only know what he told—but this boy said it was so. He said that barber reached down underneath and opened a door and pulled out somethin'. He said it looked like dice in a jar, but he guessed it weren't dice. And the barber took and shuck 'em and took 'em out and rubbed 'em on his hands and said a couple words. He said he didn't understand what they were 'cause he was a child. And them warts started goin' away till finally he got rid of every wart.

And there was another man—he's dead now too—and he says his nose used to bleed an awful lot. A lot of people used to have trouble with their nose bleedin' for no reason. Not too many people have that now either.

He said this man told his mother, says, "You know the red corn like you hang up—only the red. If you can get somebody to string red corn on a string and put it on that child's neck—let him wear it—his nose will stop, and he will never have any more trouble."

She says she couldn't do it, but she got somebody to string it, and he wore it. He says his nose stopped, and he never had no more trouble. And he said—of course they sold the home now—it was still hangin' up there, case if he ever needed it again. Now what in the world did red corn have doin' with that, but he said it was true.

∞

Her name was the *Sarah Conaway*, and she was a cargo boat. Captain Evans had her tied up down at the wharf. This old man from down in North Carolina used to go with him; his name was Pete Drinkwater. The old man had no family, you know, but he had this dog, and that dog stayed on there with him all the time.

Some tug boat captain was bringin' up some barges this day, and he was drunk. He was over too far, and he hit the *Sarah Conaway* and broke her loose. The old man was on there, and the first thing he thought of, I guess, was his dog. He grabbed his dog up and held her. The boat drifted on down toward the old bridge, and she sunk. The old man drowned, and when they found him, his arms were still holdin' his dog.

∞

Patty Cannon's Skull

It was a pleasant morning, and finding the Dover Public Library from U. S. Route 13 was easier than I had expected. It stands amid brick buildings that have an air of history about them, a few blocks from old Dover Square and near Woodburn, Delaware's governor's mansion. Inside, two or three scattered patrons were quietly busy at their literary tasks. I introduced myself to the young man behind the desk and informed him that I had come to see "the skull."

"Oh sure," he said, and disappeared for a moment into an inner room, returning with a red hatbox, which he placed on the counter in front of me.

"Is there someone I can talk to about this?" I asked.

He pointed to where an elbow was protruding from behind a stack of books: "The director," he said, "Mr. Wetherall."

I picked up the container by its handle and walked toward the elbow, which I soon discovered was attached to a gentleman with a pleasant smile. I introduced myself again and explained why I had come.

"Has there ever been a forensic study done?" I asked.

"I don't believe so," Bob Wetherall responded. "I don't believe it's ever been run past the state pathologist or anything like that. It's obviously somebody's skull and very well may have come from the place where they said it did, but there is a lot of doubt; it's only word of mouth. Have you seen it?"

"No. I just picked her up before I joined you."

Wetherall ran the zipper around the container and flipped

open the lid. Lifting out a small cardboard carton and laying it aside on the table, he smiled and said, "These are some extra little parts."

There, resting on a cushion of red velvet and displaying what could very well be the ravages of a former burial and the passing of a hundred and seventy years, sat "Patty Cannon's skull." The cranium was missing its mandible, and there were no teeth that I could immediately observe. A large portion of the bone between the nose and the left eye socket was missing. A hasty, mostly uneducated appraisal of the sutures indicated that the owner was not a young person at the time of death.

"I came here in 1989," Wetherall explained. "Mrs. Batton, who was the director for many years, had written a piece about the library for the tercentennial reviews, and I thought I would read that. When I saw this, I said, 'We have Patty Cannon's skull?' They said, 'Sure,' and handed me the hatbox. It was supposed to be loaned to us by Alfred Joseph, who was Dover City Engineer at one time, but he is long since dead."

Wetherall removed a document which had been tucked in next to the brain case, unfolded it, and handed it to me. Neatly typed on the letter-sized sheet was this narrative:

Just after the turn of the century James Marsh (my uncle by marriage) was reading law in the office of Robert White of Georgetown, Delaware. Since during this apprenticeship period there was little income he took the position of deputy sheriff of Sussex County. While holding this job the bodies of Patty Cannon and one or two others who had been buried in the jail yard of the Sussex Jail were exhumed for reburial in potters field. The yard now is a parking lot and is south of the old jail which is now the Sussex County Board of Assessment Building.

In 1827 Patty had taken arsenic and died while being held for trial for murder. [Patty Cannon actually died in the Georgetown Jail in 1829.]

Somehow while moving these bodies Patty's skull came

into the possession of James Marsh.

About 1907 James Marsh contracted acute tuberculosis and in an effort to save himself moved to Denver, Colorado. At this time he gave the skull to my father, Charles I. Joseph of Angola, Sussex County for keeping. From that time until the late thirties the skull hung on a nail in a rafter of my father's barn, by which time it had become quite a curiosity. To save it from damage or possible theft he put it in a box and stored it on the attic of his home. At his death in 1946 I took possession of the skull and in 1961 put it on loan to the Dover Library.

> Alfred W. Joseph
> Dover, Delaware
> May 2, 1963

Like so many relics of this kind, Patty Cannon's skull seems to have cloned itself over the years. There is a footnote in *The Entailed Hat* which informs us that "The skull of Ebenezer Johnson can be seen at Fowler & Wells Museum. There, also, are the skulls of Patty and Betty Cannon."

The Ebenezer referred to is the senior Johnson, whose death is chronicled in the novel, and Betty, in the same chapter, is identified as Patty's sister. One wonders if this is part of Townsend's tale or an attempt to supplement it with factual information. A well-known Townsend scholar, Dr. Jerry Shields, believed that the author was not romanticizing in his footnotes and that Townsend had probably been to the museum and had seen the skulls.

We also have the claim contained in *The Narrative and Confessions of Lucretia Cannon*, which informs us that Patty's skull was obtained by a "celebrated and highly respected phrenologist" for examination, and that in 1841 it was in the possession of Mr. O. S. Fowler of Philadelphia.

The "science" of phrenology was the brainchild of a Viennese physician named Franz Joseph Gall, who, with a student, Johann Kaspar Spurzheim, in the early part of the nineteenth century spread the idea across Europe and to America, where it found its most devoted following.

Spurzheim died while touring the United States, and his banner was taken up by Orson Fowler, a ministry student said to have suddenly found his true calling. Fowler's enthusiasm infected his younger brother, Lorenzo, and together they toured the country, lecturing and analyzing the character and propensities of simple folk as well as the rich and famous by reading bumps and depressions on their craniums.

The brothers' New York office, known at one time as the "Phrenological Cabinet," became a bizarre museum. After the 1836 death of Aaron Burr, for example, they had a cast of his head commissioned and declared—as a surprise to no one—that his organs of "Secretiveness" and "Destructiveness" were far larger than those of the average person. The collection grew to some four thousand studies of famous and infamous craniums and included about three hundred skulls. S. R. Wells became a partner.

References immediately available to me provided no additional information about the collection. Before I had an opportunity to expand my investigation, however, Dr. Shields told me that he had spoken to the New York Historical Society about Fowler and Wells. The Society confirmed the depository's existence but has no record of its inventory or its eventual fate.

Is it possible that a Philadelphia phrenologist might have gained permission to remove the skull of a deceased criminal from the Sussex County jailyard? Of course it is. Fowler and Wells apparently made a practice of such collecting. Phrenology was all the rage, and at that time no laws existed to prevent it. Neither did Patty Cannon have any known relatives in the region to protest. Along with the Johnson brothers and other members of the gang, Patty's immediate family had fled south and were scattered from Florida to Texas.

Is it also possible that a deputy sheriff assigned the task of removing the remains of several former prisoners to potter's field could have "somehow" come into possession of one of the skulls? Again, the answer is yes.

Beyond a determination of sex and age, I do not know what might be learned from the Dover Library skull, but modern forensic anthropologists are capable of some remarkable sleuthing. I decided it would be interesting to have someone with the necessary knowledge take a look at the partially deteriorated cranium, but I have not been successful in raising any interest in such a project. There does not appear to be any apprehension that someone might debunk the skull; it is rather a matter of not taking it seriously to begin with. Most commonly I am told that the skull is too small to have belonged to such a large and powerful person as Patty Cannon, but was Patty Cannon a large and powerful person, or is it only her legend that has achieved that status?

I hope the artifact will someday be critically examined by an expert. Meanwhile, I think that the Fowler and Wells version stands a better chance of being authentic.

Another study should be conducted to answer the question of whether Fowler included an evaluation of Patty Cannon's skull in his writings? Phrenological journals from the period would seem to be the logical place to begin the search.

Occasionally a journalist still seeks out the Dover Public Library with the objective of meeting Patty Cannon face to face. Among the national publications which have demonstrated an interest in the notorious lady and her legend is *Readers Digest,* and the red hatbox once journeyed to Wilmington, where it commanded the center of attention in a television interview. Actually it was the late Dr. Jerry Shields who was interviewed; Patty had nothing to say.

On special occasions the library staff has placed the somewhat grizzly artifact on public display, usually around Halloween. If you happen to be in the area and express an interest in Patty to the library staff, they will probably allow you to peek into the hatbox. If any reader is an authority or a student in the matter of old bones and would consider contributing a little time to attempting a solution of one of Del-

The Author Contemplates Patty Cannon's Skull
Photo by Brice Stump

marva's long-standing mysteries, give me a call; I'd like to be there when you meet "the wickedest woman ever to walk on American soil."

∞

Kendall run a barber shop out the old blacksmith place. They used to shoe horses in there and all that stuff. He cut hair and bootlegged some along with it, and then he bought fish and all kinds of game and sold that too. You'd be settin' in the chair and him shavin' you, and some fellow would come in and want a fish. He'd stop and wrap up a fish for the man, and then he'd start back to shavin' you again, and he never would even wipe his hands.

To start with, you're not supposed to sell geese and ducks and them things no way, not even back then. He had some loose boards in the floor in the back, and people would put ducks in there. A fella would come in the night and pick 'em up and leave the money in a box in there.

I used to get my hair cut in Cambridge. I only went to Kendall one time. He shaved me one time, and he shaved me twice—the first and the last. That razor—I ain't lyin' to you now—I've seen plenty of people, when they used to butcher hogs, they had that knife and scraped the hair off. Well, those knives was a lot sharper than that razor was. It pulled the hair out and everything else. He was liable to take his razor and shuck an oyster with it—anything. Now don't put who said this in your book or it might start trouble. Some of his gang might be still livin'.

∞

Don't
Encourage Him

"**I** am not a shy person," John Root Hopkins announced to a gridlocked audience in Troika Gallery on the opening night of his show; "nor am I humble.

"I was painting one night, and the devil came to me and said, 'John, I hear you complain that you don't have this skill or that skill, and you don't know this medium and that medium. I will give you the talent you want.'

"I said, 'Well, knowing you, you'll want something in return.'

"And he said, 'Yes, I'd like your soul.'

"I said, 'It ain't worth a lot, but I just can't do that.'

"So I've taken what I have—mean as it is—and done a lot with it. Again, no modesty intended.

"I do different art. I do social commentary like 'Salome' [a larger-than-life portrait of Secretary of State Madeleine Albright holding the head of Saddam Hussein on a platter] and 'American Mecca' [rows of supplicants prostrating themselves before a minaret with the word 'Fat' emblazoned on it]. I think America likes fat," the artist observed; "I like fat.

"And I do primitive things like cats or cows or pigs or ships. I do them in a primitive style because I really don't have the talent that the devil offered me.

"I do whimsical things like 'Little Red Riding Hood' and 'Noah's Ark' with Mickey Mouse and Minnie Mouse and some awful pictures [his face lit up with a mischievous expression]

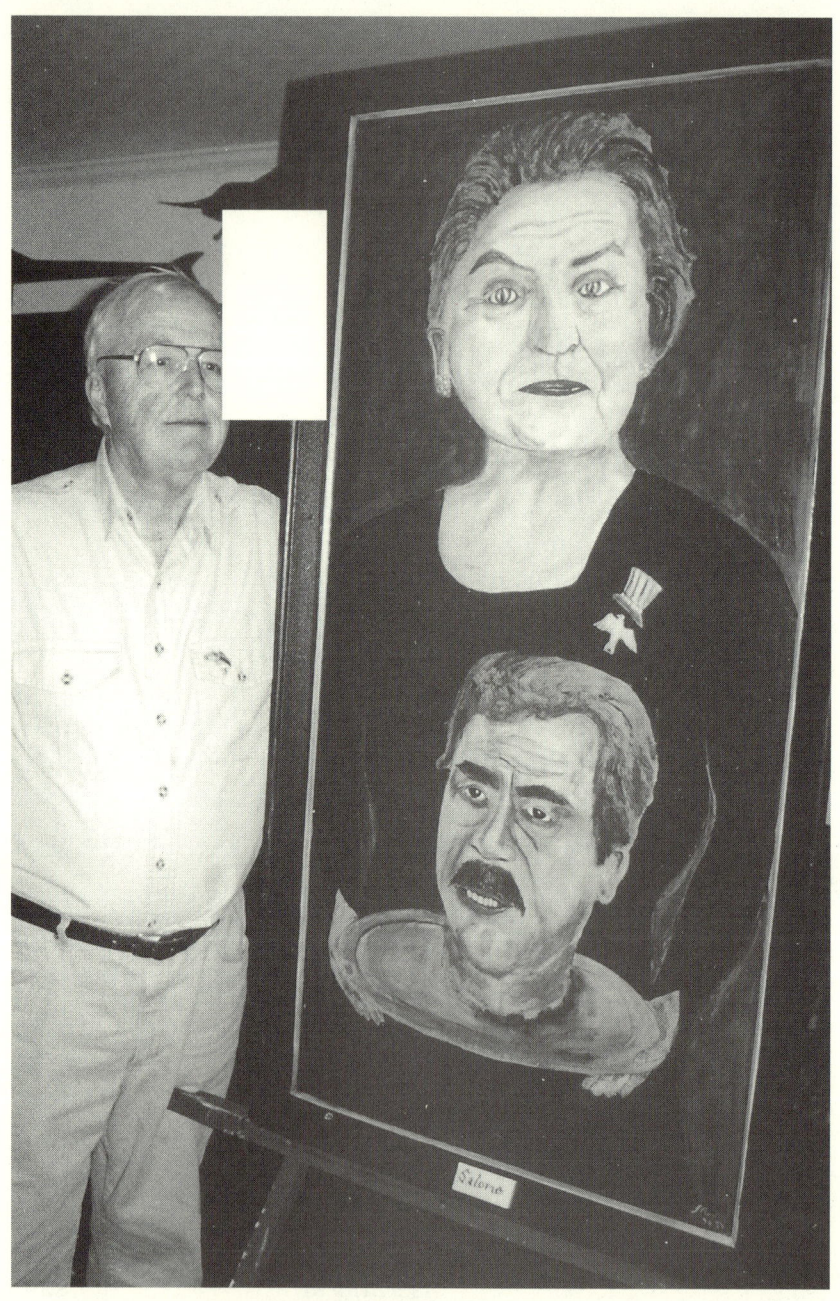

John Root Hopkins and "Salome"

called 'Reveling with Harlots' and 'Consorting' and 'Adam and Eve.'

"I have concluded that that's what I do and that I should be happy to do even that, and I intend to continue to do that and try to sell it.

"The thing I want to say through my art is, 'Hey, stay loose. Don't get all up tight. Have some fun.' And I do. I enjoy my painting immensely, but I must tell you that none of it comes easily. I struggle and I goof up."

I had heard that some of the creations of this "self-taught itinerant with a southern heritage," as Hopkins labels himself, have hung in the National Gallery, the Phillips, the Corcoran, the Tate, the Chicago Institute, the Louvre—more than a dozen internationally celebrated galleries—where the artist has mounted his miniatures with duct tape in restroom stalls while visiting.

"That janitorial help stole the pieces shortly thereafter," the painter will tell you with an expression of sobriety, "is of no moment to this arresting fact."

"You didn't really do that?" I chided, while visiting this remarkable man at his lovely old farmhouse on Lee Creek near Cambridge.

"It's a true story," he responded; "I really did that."

When Hopkins graduated from VMI in 1952, the United Nations was at war in Korea. He quickly joined the fray, assigned as a forward observer, directing artillery fire and flying on missions to guide napalm air strikes.

"On our side," he is quick to point out.

"One of the greatest moments of my life," Hopkins recalled, "was to fire corps artillery. That's every gun in the corps—over two hundred. Boom!" he mimicked the blast, still donning, after nearly fifty years, an expression of awe when savoring the memory. "Big boom!"

When the Chinese mounted one of their drives and pushed our troops back toward the 38th parallel, Hopkins' unit was overrun. Failing to follow his advice to stick to the high ground, his men were captured. He escaped.

"I enjoyed the service," he admits, "even though I was scared [bleep]less most of the time. It was a high point—a defining moment in my life."

A long, high, stairway wall in Hopkins' home—he calls it his "ego wall"—is covered by a vast collection of diplomas, appointments, patents, certificates, and awards from his many careers and activities. Almost lost among them is a framed silver star, awarded for combat heroism.

Hopkins' life has been a kaleidoscope of careers and honors and adventures: researcher; sales engineer; examiner in the U. S. Patent Office; recipient of LLB and J.D. degrees from George Washington University Law School; attorney for the Association of American Railroads; patent attorney; member of various Federal bars, including the bar of the U. S. Supreme Court; member of the American Patent Law Association, the American Bar Association, and the Federal Bar Association; development engineer; inventor of thirteen U. S. and numerous foreign patents; corporate executive with responsibilities in the U. S., England, France, Italy, and Spain; author and commentator—the list goes on and on.

Hopkins retired from a vice president's position with the world's largest maker of electrical connectors in 1986 and traveled around the world for two years—"playing," he says. Then he went back to work as a patent consultant. He retired again in 1993 to write a book about business. Presently he serves as director for two Delaware corporations, is chairman of the Tax Board of Appeals in his county of residence, writes social and political commentary, and paints. Some retirement!

"I've been painting all along," this Renaissance man told me, "even before high school. It was a little bit here and a little bit there. In the eighties I started painting more and was encouraged because I won some prizes.

"In the first contest I won," Hopkins related, "the painting was called 'Brig in Port.' It was a big ship—a marvelous picture. I took that painting into the little antique shop I had at the time and marked it six hundred dollars.

"A woman who ran another shop came in with her husband and tried to beat me down—offered me three hundred. I said, 'No, no, no,' and she went away. In those days I tried to do at least three hundred dollars of business a week. I had to do that to cover expenses. That week I hadn't sold anything, and I was desperate. On Sunday afternoon she came back and offered me three and a quarter, and so I let her beat me down.

"Her husband picked up the painting while she was writing the check. I still had the first place ribbon on there, and he took the ribbon.

"I said, 'Hey, look, whoa! That's my ego. That's my personal honor. You can't have that.' I went on a little bit.

"The woman said, 'Ten dollars?'

"I said, 'Sold!'

"I learned later that she resold the painting for a thousand dollars or more.

"One year I had my own art show. I had my house full of paintings, and I invited Laura Era and Dorothy Newland to judge the show. I won first, second, third, fourth, fifth, sixth, seventh . . . honorable mention, best in show. I had a wonderful time. I had a band come and play. I hired some little girls from the ballet school, and they danced. I just had a marvelous time. That was two or three years ago, and I've kept painting. Now I'm in a phase where painting is my main thing.

"I go to a lot of art shows. I went to nineteen museums last year. I go, and I see, and I learn. I'm not promising that I'm going to continue to paint—I may get bored—but for now I'm having fun."

In addition to his conventional paintings (if you can call any of his images that), Hopkins makes whimsical animals of wood—cats and fish mostly. He has done Dorchester County mosquitoes, some carrying bombs beneath their wings, others mounting machine guns.

A Collection of John Root Paintings

A huge painting of a "vosprey"—a cross between a vulture and an osprey—has lighted eyes, and there are portraits with clock mechanisms mounted behind the head to make the eyes move.

He has done "flap paintings." When the flap is down, the painting appears to be one thing. Raised, it becomes another. One depicts a Value Jet airliner. Moving the flap displays a rubber-band motor. Another of a fisherman peacefully pursuing his pastime becomes a totally different scene when the flap is raised, exposing a shark about to devour the luckless Isaac Walton.

Once he startled neighbors by towing a three-dimensional shark behind his sailboat.

A large sculpture constructed of glued styrofoam panels, which Hopkins intended to fiberglass for permanency, was left on the lawn while he made a trip to town for more glue. A storm hit while he was away and blew the object into the creek. "That was the end of that," he said with a shrug. "It came all to pieces."

Among his cat-food-can paintings is a collection of empty containers attached in rows to a board. Inside the cans, on their bottoms, are portraits of pigs in a variety of professions.

"These are macaroons," he said, showing me a strange-looking piece—cookies glued on a pair of eye glasses. "I don't know why I did that; I was probably drinking."

"Jack the Reaper," an oversized painting of Dr. Kevorkian holding an actual scythe, leers from a corner of his studio. And there is a life-sized cutout of Big Liz, the famous headless ghost of Greenbriar Swamp.

He has made paintings in boxes.

The rendition of a crab eating a DNR officer was his gift to a waterman.

"Sometimes I use discretion," Hopkins said at one point. I forget the object of our discussion at the moment.

"But not often," I countered.

"No, not often," he agreed.

There is a painting depicting the French-fries war between MacDonalds and Burger King, another called "Prophesy," which shows the dirigible Hindenburg exploding, and a copy of a Jamie Wyeth original. There are paintings of Creatins—yes, Creatins—and he has written a book titled *The History of Creatins.* Ask him to explain it.

Hopkins rambled from room to room, exhibiting his delight in the prized art and books and photographs and other objects which fill his home and studio.

"That's my great-grandfather Isaac Stiles, taken in 1868," my guide pointed to a portrait. "He was president of Emory and the first president of Georgia Tech."

A college professor acting as judge for an art show once awarded Hopkins a first place ribbon, then candidly remarked in his critique, "This artist obviously doesn't have any drawing talent, but the thing looks like it's two hundred years old, and that's why I gave it the prize."

"So from then on," Hopkins admitted to me, "I started making my paintings look old."

He generally paints with acrylics, then applies many coats of varnish and shellac, and completes the aging process with a wipe of aniline dye. "I learned that from my father-in-law," he remarked. "He was a cabinet maker."

Hopkins signs his work "J. Root."

"Why your middle name?" I asked.

"Well, you need a name," he responded, "and that's easy."

"Root" is a family name. A great uncle who bore it and died in 1890 was an acclaimed architect who designed many homes and public buildings throughout the country.

Scattered on a sideboard in Hopkins' kitchen, where he frequently works, I observed dozens of caricatures drawn on card stock. These he colors by hand and distributes to lucky acquaintances. Most are outrageous commentaries on a wide variety of things.

Several friends have urged him to duplicate the cards for sale. "The cards are for fun." Hopkins said. "I have hundreds, and I keep doing them. I want to be deemed slightly crazy. People are afraid of crazy people."

Five times Hopkins has entered the muskrat cook-off and twice placed second in the Outdoor Show at Golden Hill. "Root's Rat Pie" took honors one year; in another he placed with his "MacRat Burgers."

"I offered it to MacDonalds," he told me soberly, "but for some reason they turned it down." Hopkins' muskrat recipes can be found in his book, *Muskrat Cookin'*.

"Once," he said, "when I was on my muskrat kick, I took a rat and displayed it in various poses: having its hair cut, reading the Bible, in a coffin. . . ."

A major heart attack in 1981, a bypass operation in 1992, diabetes, and a stroke in 1998 have not appreciably slowed

Hopkins down. "I do get tired," he admitted, "and I take a nap most afternoons. Half an hour will do."

"What do you want people to remember about you?" I asked as I was preparing to leave. "Finish this inscription for me: 'Here lies John Root Hopkins. . . .'"

There was a long, sober pause, the most serious moment in the two hours we had been together. Finally he replied, "He lived life to the fullest."

And, indeed, John Root Hopkins has allowed no moss to grow on his backside. His wife, however, once suggested a different epitaph: "Don't encourage him!"

Self Portrait on a John Root Greeting Card

∞

"Crazy" Dow
A Modern Elijah

I doubt that the thought ever invaded his wildest dreams —of which he had many—that nearly two centuries after his death, legions of family researchers would puzzle over finding his name on their genealogical charts. By 1820 there were literally thousands of Lorenzo Dows scattered across America, and, as the man himself slowly sank into historical obscurity, they in turn became namesakes for their own descendants.

Through the latitude of modern media we have been exposed to an assortment of ministers representing one gospel or another, but how, we must wonder, could a poor, eccentric, wandering preacher, a man who was not even ordained by an organized religion, manage to access the majority of Americans and gain such an audience and reputation that thousands of babies were named for him? The simple answer lies in the horse, and it was on the back of one that he blazed his mark across every state of our then young nation.

Lorenzo Dow was born on October 16, 1777, in Coventry, Connecticut, the descendant of English ancestors. He was an asthmatic child, and poor health continued to dog him throughout his life. After nearly dying of smallpox on a trip to Ireland early in his career, he remained thereafter a gaunt and emaciated figure.

When young Lorenzo was only three years old, he began

to experience the awakening influences of religion, but it was in his thirteenth year that he had several dreams which led him to a state of deep conviction.

Of one of these visions he later wrote, "I knew I was unprepared to die . . . and I again resolved to seek the salvation of my soul. I began that day to pray in secret, but how to pray or what to pray for, I scarcely knew. I at once broke off from all my old companions and evil practices, which some call innocent mirth, and betook to the Bible, kneeling in private. I frequently felt, for a few seconds, cords of sweet love to draw me on, but from whence it flowed, I could not tell. I since believe it was for an encouragement to hope in the mercy of God."

Shortly afterward he became troubled with thoughts that he might be predestined to be lost, and he resolved to destroy his own life. His mind was changed, however, when he attended a Methodist meeting.

During one of the sermons the preacher accidentally pointed his finger towards the youth and exclaimed, "Sinner, there is a frowning Providence above your head and a burning hell beneath your feet, and nothing but the brittle thread of life prevents your soul from falling into endless perdition. If you don't pray, then you'll be damned!"

This message, he said, came to his heart like a dagger, and he felt afraid to move, lest he should tumble into hell. He went home that night and prayed, then dreamed he was carried off to hell by a devil.

On awaking, he prayed fervently: "Lord, I give up; I submit; I yield. If there be mercy in heaven for me, let me know it, and if not, let me go down to hell and know the worst of my case."

As he spoke these words, an answer came to his mind: "Son! thy sins are forgiven thee. Thy faith hath saved thee. Go in peace."

"The burden of sin and guilt and the fear of hell vanished from my mind," Dow later wrote. "Daylight dawned. I arose and went out of doors, and everything I cast my eye upon seemed to be speaking forth the praise and wonders of the Almighty. It appeared more like a new world than anything else I can compare it to."

In 1796 Dow applied unsuccessfully for admission to the Connecticut Methodist Conference, but continued to press his claim and was finally admitted on trial in September, 1798. Within a year he had been shuffled between posts in New York, Massachusetts, and Vermont, and during that time developed what he felt to be a divine conviction to preach to Roman Catholics.

Hearing that Ireland was the greatest Catholic stronghold, he requested a leave of absence to make a trip abroad. The request was denied, and against the advice and entreaties of his superiors, he embarked for Europe late in 1799 and there preached the gospel incessantly to a reluctant Irish Catholic audience, especially directing his crusade against the Jesuits, whom he denounced as enemies to pure religion and to republican government. Eccentricities of dress and speech often led crowds to jeer him.

Notwithstanding the fact that he had made the European tour against the authority of the Conference, he resumed preaching upon his return the following year and remained on trial, but it was not long before the discontented reverend and his disappointed conference parted company.

Although Dow was never ordained to the ministry and therefore lacked authority to administer sacrament or organize societies, he remained a Methodist in doctrinal principles and continued to promulgate the prominent doctrines of Methodism throughout his life. Once asked to what particular religious faith or doctrine he adhered, he replied, "I am Methodist chain and Quaker filling."

In 1805 he revisited England and Ireland and instituted the camp meeting, an innovation that led to controversy and resulted in the organization of the Primitive Methodists in England.

Dow then took up the calling as an itinerant minister and began to restlessly traverse the country on horseback, probing particularly into the south and west, where he was sometimes the first ever to preach a sermon.

Primarily drawn to small villages, this expounder of the Lord's word often attracted the entire population. Frequently he announced the dates he would preach a year in advance and kept them faithfully. It is likely that more Americans heard Lorenzo Dow deliver a sermon than any other minister of his day.

On his long journeys he preferred camping out at night, especially in pine woods, where he would gather huge piles of shats to make his bed. With such a lifestyle, staying well-groomed was a problem, and Dow often arrived at his destinations looking like a wild man.

Upon entering a village, he would mount a stump or take possession of a street corner and begin to proclaim what he called his mission from God: to preach the gospel to every creature. His habit of dashing into a community, dismounting, and immediately commencing to exhort with fire and fervor gained him the common designation of "Crazy Dow," though he preferred the title "Son of Thunder" or "The Cosmopolite." He was considered by many to be a modern Elijah.

It was the prevalent opinion during his lifetime that he was a man of unsound mind, and that view detracted from the effect of his eloquence. Nevertheless, his power as an orator reached out and touched the utmost borders of civilization in the young nation.

Dow was a restless dreamer, contradictory, and never happier than when engaged in a war of words. Though he possessed a scant formal education, gained entirely in a small district school, he was a close and discriminating observer of mankind. Though poor and ill-provided for by his itinerant ministry, it is said that he often gave what he had to others in financial difficulty.

Lorenzo Dow never remained long in any one location, but

he left a lasting impact in every community he visited. His was a time when public speakers were expected to motivate people to tears and to hysteria, and he was acknowledged to be among the best at stirring passions. Members of his audience were often moved to the point of "jerking," an uncontrollable physical reaction to his oratory, and many later claimed they had been touched by God.

He has been described as a "large, stoop-shouldered, and raw-honed man." His face was rough, yet contained delicate, almost effeminate features, and many of those who saw him said it was marked by a radiant, indomitable energy, tempered with the light of kindness. His beard reached to his waist, and his hair, parted in the middle, was loose and flowing to his shoulders.

> Loose his beard, and hoary hair
> Streamed like a meteor to the troubled air.

Joshua Thomas, known affectionately on Chesapeake Bay as "The Parson of the Islands," called Dow "the most singular-looking man I ever saw," but the parson's first impression of the flamboyant evangelist was not a positive one. Writing about a service he had attended, Thomas related: "Lorenzo Dow was preaching very powerful, when a woman in the congregation became excited and happy and started up shouting aloud. The preacher cried out, 'The Lord is here! He is with that sister.' I immediately jumped upon my feet to see the Lord, but I could not see him, and concluded within myself: 'This cannot be true, for I can see as well as he can, and I do not see him. That man must be one of these deceivers.'"

Dow was a well known figure on Delmarva. While touring Maryland in 1805, he exhorted to more than two thousand devotees in Pocomoke City, then called Newton. On his way to preach, the flamboyant orator is said to have encountered an African American boy carrying a tin horn. He employed the young man to climb an ancient elm tree on the meeting ground and to remain absolutely still there until a point in the sermon when Dow would loudly exclaim, "Blow, Gabriel, blow!" At this command the boy was to put every bit of breath he could muster into making the horn do its work.

The sermon was a fierce admonishment on the subject of the Resurrection and the Day of Judgment. Finally reaching his climax and describing the Angel Gabriel as standing with one foot on the sea and the other upon the land—his long, silver trumpet in hand—Dow shouted, "Blow, Gabriel, blow!" and was immediately obeyed. And just as instantly, pandemonium broke upon the meeting. The congregation fell to the ground, shouting salvation and crying for mercy. Horses squealed and stampeded. Then someone spotted the boy with the horn in the elm tree, and the shamed sinners turned threateningly on Dow. He was equal to the occasion. "If a little boy can strike such terror into your hearts," he shouted, "what will you do when the great day really comes?"

This man of God was never above the use of subterfuge to make his point. On another occasion, when someone complained of the theft of several iron wedges used to split rails, Dow asked to borrow a similar item. In the middle of his meeting that afternoon, with everyone shouting and praying, the preacher picked up the borrowed tool, and, rearing back as if to hurl the heavy implement, he shouted, "May God carry this straight to the head of the man that stole our brother's wedges." Everybody looked confused, except for one fellow a few rows back, who ducked. "There's the guilty man," said Dow, and the culprit confessed and begged forgiveness.

There is a tale told in the governor's mansion in Dover, Delaware, that Dow was once the guest of its third owner and frightened his host's family when he related to them his meeting with a stranger on Woodburn's great stairway. There was no other guest in the house at the time.

In his wonderful historical novel about Delmarva, *The*

Entailed Hat, George Alfred Townsend relates an encounter at a Pungoteague camp meeting between Dow and King Custis, which resulted in Dow placing a curse on the Custis family. Claims Townsend, Dow pointed his finger at Custis and his wife and shouted, "The lord shall smite thee, whited sepulcher, and mock thee in thy children's children, thou Ahab and thy Jezebel." All this because Custis behaved poorly during Dow's sermon.

During another of his sermons Dow addressed the women present, many of whom were decked out in the latest fashion of their day. "Here you are," he bellowed, "curled, crimped, ringed, bobbed, and feathered. How the devil will make them feathers fly when he gets you."

On another occasion, confronted by a group of attorneys in the audience, he leaned over the railing at the close of his sermon and addressed them directly, saying:

If a lawyer you would be
You must learn to lie and cheat,
For lawyers, not like other men
Have honest bread to eat.

Then the quaint circuit rider jumped out of the window, mounted his horse, and galloped out of town without speaking to another person.

Entering another settlement and finding a Presbyterian church crowned by a cupola, Dow raised himself in the saddle and shouted, "Ah, the devil has been here before me. See that church with a steeple. That church is built in honor of the devil." Then dismounting, he hitched his horse on a street corner and commenced his harangue.

Dow traveled in every state of the Union—seventeen at the time—as well as in Canada, England, Ireland, and Wales. His wife Peggy, whom he married in 1804, accompanied him on many of his travels. Their only child was born in Ireland and died in England. After Peggy died on January 6,

1820, he married Lucy Dolbeare in the same year.

Dow's meticulously kept journal was published after his death, in 1859, as *History of the Cosmopolite, or the Writings of Rev. Lorenzo Dow.*

The Reverend Dow died on February 2, 1834. A plain slab of sandstone, upon which his name is inscribed, marks his resting place in the city cemetery of Georgetown, District of Columbia.

∞

There used to be a blacksmith shop in there, and he was a pretty good blacksmith. On Sunday he would go around town and carry the Sunday paper. One day he was almost finished, and somebody came along and asked him to go somewhere in a car. I was just a little old boy. He said, "Boy, you take this paper over to Mr. Tom's place and set it on his porch, and you be careful you don't drop it." I thought, "Hell, it won't hurt nothin' if I drop a paper." So he got in the car and went on, and I carried it over there. It was heavy for a paper, and I said, "There's somethin' in there." I opened it up, and he had a half pint of bootleg whiskey in there. He had a little still upstairs in the blacksmith shop, and he had four or five customers, and every Sunday he would deliver a half pint with their paper. That was a long time ago—in the early twenties.

∞

Return
of the Trumpeters

Christened Lavinia, history honors her as "Lovey" Lake, daughter of Henry Lake, a company commander during the American Revolution and later State's Judge and High Sheriff. Through commonly accepted tradition she endures as one of the cherished legends of Dorchester County, Maryland.

To my knowledge, no record of the date has been preserved on which a contingent of British soldiers and Tories attempted to take Captain Lake into custody. Landing on the shores of the Honga River, they surprised the household, but the Lake women were more than equal to the challenge. Firmly grasping her husband, Rhoda Lake struggled with several British soldiers and was subdued only after being wounded with a bayonet. Lovey, an attractive, spirited teenager, became incensed at the British for their treatment of her parents and for attempting to remove the silver buckles from her shoes. She was so defiant they threw her into another room and set fire to the dwelling. Quickly extinguishing the flames, Lovey dashed out the back door and ran to alert nearby members of her father's company, who arrived in time to rescue him.

As I headed toward Crapo to meet with Bob Ferris and V. K. Holtzendorf to discuss the first stages of a project designed to reestablish the trumpeter swan on the Atlantic Flyway, I had no idea I would be spending the morning in the very house where pertinacious Lovey was born and grew to womanhood, and in the very room where she defied the Crown of England.

Lake Cove Farm

Trumpeter swans, the largest of North American waterfowl, had been absent from Delmarva for two centuries, having been extirpated by a combination of hunting and feather collecting and the agricultural conversion of wetlands. Before measures were finally taken to save them, the race had been reduced to sixty-nine individuals in the contiguous states.

Bob Ferris, Director of the Species Conservation Division for Defenders of Wildlife, told me he was just beginning to feel the full impact of the project he was then heading in partnership with Dr. William Sladen, director of Environmental Studies at the Airlie Center near Warrenton, Virginia.

Waterfowl tend to accept as their parent the first large, mobile object they encounter after hatching. This phenomenon, known as imprinting, can begin with sounds the chick hears while still in its shell.

In the spring of 1997 three clutches of trumpeter eggs were hatched at Airlie, where the eight survivors were taught to fly with their surrogate parents, two ultralight aircraft to which they had been imprinted. The objective of the biologists was to entice the little flock to follow the ultralights to Crapo in the fall and to have them migrate on their own back to Airlie in the spring.

"We're doing this hundred-mile migration," Ferris told me, "not because we're trying to set up a migration path between Crapo and Airlie, but because we don't know if it's going to work, and it's better to first try something which is tightly controlled. If they return to Virginia, that's the end for this part of the project. All of the birds will have radio collars on them, so if some birds don't migrate, we can correct it."

If the swans should succeed in learning this short route, a larger flock would be trucked to a training site in New York or Ontario in the spring of 1998, and that base would then serve as a launching pad for a longer trial.

"What happens after that?" I asked.

"We'll do it again," Ferris said. "The ultimate objective is to reestablish the trumpeter on the Atlantic Flyway."

Many people have contributed to blazing the trail in advance of the trumpeter project, including Bill Lishman, who conducted the migration training endeavor with Canada geese, which was depicted in the popular, fictionalized movie, *Fly Away Home.*

"Few people understand," Ferris offered, "the strange pathway this project has taken as far as connections with the past are concerned. Dr. Eckhart Hess bought this farm in the sixties, and here he conducted the seminal American research on waterfowl imprinting. Hess was a colleague of Conrad Lorenz (the European pioneer in imprinting research) before he came here. Dr. Sladen was also a colleague of Lorenz. No one could have predicted that all of this was going to happen:

that V. K. and I would buy this farm where the original imprinting was done, which has really good habitat for the project, and that we would come to work with Bill Sladen, who
has taken the Hess research and continued it as his passion."

Long before the hour was out, I had absorbed Bob's and
V. K.'s enthusiasm and was hooked. I could hardly wait for
the crisp autumn morning when two ultralight "parents"
would buzz in from the Honga River, leading their little flock
of eager "children" back to a land that has played such a
large role in the heritage of their species.

Nearly ten human generations had been laid to rest since
a trumpeter's mellow, high-pitched coo had echoed across
Lake Cove. Lavinia, our feisty young heroine, was among the
last to know them as more than just a myth. I am not usually a spiritual person, but as I drove home through the lush
marshes of South Dorchester that day, I hoped that somehow
Lovey would be there with me, and Eckhart Hess, too.

Chased by a slightly bulging half-moon, the constellation
Orion had just disappeared into the western woods the next
time I left for Lake Cove. Only a hint of gray smeared the eastern horizon, where the sun would soon deliver a new day and
erase the frost that overnight had turned field and wood into a sparkling fairyland.

As each mile hummed by, the light over my left shoulder
increased. Several bands of clouds suspended just above the
horizon evolved from dark, gray umbrellas into rainbows of
crimson, orange, and saffron, through tints and shades for
which only artists know the names.

At Blackwater National Wildlife Refuge I pulled over for a
few enraptured seconds. The whole eastern panorama of sky
and water was aflame—interrupted here and there by the
black masses of loblolly-mantled islands.

But I dared not tarry. I can view sunrise almost any morning, but no man had watched a trumpeter swan slide down
an autumn wind in Maryland for nearly two hundred years.

In one hour, several of these magnificent birds would be returning to the Chesapeake Bay.

My e-mail the day before had brought tantalizing tidbits of news:

At 7:30 a.m. three female trumpeters—Isabelle, Yoyo, and Sydney—were airborne out of Auburn, Virginia, accompanied by two ultralight aircraft, one captained by Gavin Shire, biologist at Airlie, the second by Joe Duff from Operation Migration. Shire and Duff were the actual aviators in the popular film *Fly Away Home*.

By 8:50 a.m. the strange-looking flock had crossed the Potomac. The mission was going so well, my monitor informed me, that Shire had overflown the first scheduled landing and would continue to Buds Ferry before taking a break.

At 3:11 p.m. the swans were again airborne and proceeding to Magruders Ferry on the Patuxent River, where they would spend the night. Only the Chesapeake now stood between them and their wintering grounds in Dorchester County.

Since Canadian sculptor and aviator William Lishman first demonstrated the technique in 1986, geese and sandhill cranes have been successfully taught preselected migration routes, and in 1997 three endangered whooping cranes accompanied a flock of sandhills for the first time. Waterfowl have to be shown a migration route from the air before they can repeat it. When there are no adult birds to accomplish that, experiments have demonstrated that man and the ultralight can successfully serve as proxies.

Lake Cove Farm was bustling with activity when I arrived. The crisp air crackled with expectation and cell-phone news. The pilots were up, defrosting their ultralights. There would be a short delay before the birds became airborne. In the center of the bay a Coast Guard cutter was standing by—just in case.

An hour ticked by slowly before someone transmitted the information that sight contact had been made with the cutter. Reporters, photographers, and project team members took up positions along the landing strip. A billowing wind sock announced a stiffening breeze coming off the Honga River. A cross wind would increase the difficulty of the approach and landing.

A few more expectant moments and someone announced, "Seven minutes out!" I cupped my hands behind my ears to be the first to pick up the muted, mosquito-like buzz of the ultralights.

Then, "There they are!"

Trumpeter Swans Return to Delmarva

In tight formation, pumping short, almost effortless wing strokes in the eddies of air behind the lead plane's wing, three majestic young trumpeters bore directly into the sun's glare. Banking in a wide arc, the unlikely squadron circled for a better view and feel of the geography and wind.

On the ground every eye was on the swans, tied by an invisible bond of devotion to surrogate mom Gavin Shire.

Then, as the biologist's ultralight slowed and banked into its approach, one of the swans overflew it and became entangled in a stabilizing wire on top of the wing. It was Yoyo, the most curious and affectionate of the cygnets. Shortly after hatching she had endeared herself by forming a temporary bond with Bob Ferris' white sneakers.

Yoyo Caught in a Stabilizing Wire

I held my breath—seconds that seemed like an eternity—until bird and machine separated, and Yoyo plummeted toward the ground.

A team member shouted encouragement to the struggling swan. Gradually she leveled off and rejoined her sisters.

The ultralight made another wide circle, seeming to float on its broad, swept-back wing.

Just beyond the edge of the field, Shire again banked into

his approach, and again Yoyo made contact with the wing and dropped off, twisting in the air—falling.

Again shouts of encouragement rose from the field. To the relief of thirty pounding hearts, the swan recovered her stability a few yards above the ground and pumped her powerful wings to regain altitude.

Yoyo Plummets toward the Ground

Shire touched down—short because of the cross wind—and braked to a stop, the nose of his French-made Cosmos penetrating the brush at the end of the runway and scattering several photographers.

Two of the swans and Joe Duff followed Shire in, while Yoyo remained aloft.

Unbuckling himself and running to the center of the field, pilot-biologist-mom Shire called to the circling bird. Another wide swing, then one more, and in she came—stately, eight-

Sydney Follows Joe Duff to a Safe Landing

foot wings breaking her graceful descent and two black feet extending to meet the wet grass.

The roar of applause may well have been heard on Hoopers Island. Yoyo shook herself, strutted, then looked around as if to say, "What's all the fuss?"

Camera shutters clicked, camcorders whirred, and hearts gradually returned to a normal cadence.

Buckets of water and shelled corn were offered to the swans, and they were led off for a short swim in the freshwater pond behind the Lake Cove residence.

And then it was time for champagne toasts and birthday wishes to Dr. Sladen—seventy-seven—who could hardly have received a better present for the occasion. As team members and guests gathered around a picnic table, I looked up to see the swans waddling across the lawn to join us.

"With tongue in cheek," offered Roger Schlickeisen, President of Defenders of Wildlife: "The trumpeters have landed. One small step for Defenders of Wildlife and Environmental Studies at Airlie, but one giant step for waterfowl restoration on the Chesapeake Bay."

Muttering little "Yuh yuh" sounds, Yoyo reached out and pecked at Roger's trousers.

"Get his wallet!" someone in the crowd shouted.

Casting a mock scowl at the swan, Schlickeisen replied, "You've been in my wallet for months!"

After proud officials had their say, Gavin Shire raised his glass to a hushed assembly. "One final toast," the pilot who showed the way offered: "To the birds!"

Following Page Top: (Left to Right) Joe Duff, Dr. Sladen, Yoyo, Gavin Shire

Following Page Bottom: Roger Schlickeisen (Left) and Bob Ferris Congratulate Each Other on the Successful Flight

Postscript

After a relatively mild and uneventful winter, Yoyo, as might have been expected, was the first to show an inclination to migrate, and she disappeared from Lake Cove in mid March. Two weeks later she was coaxed into a fenced yard by well-meaning but uninformed residents near Patuxent River, who thought she was lost or hurt. There she was attacked by a dog and slightly injured in a gallant defense. Back at Airlie, she soon recovered.

Sydney and Isabelle tarried for several weeks longer. After crossing the Chesapeake, they became separated in bad weather, and Sydney returned to the Eastern Shore. Isabelle was collected near Centreville, Virginia, eighteen miles from Airlie.

In the summer of 1998, a new flock of nineteen birds was trucked north to prepare for migration to the Wildfowl Trust of North America's Horsehead Wetlands Center in Grasonville, Maryland.

On the morning of December 4, eleven swans divided into two flocks, each led by a pair of ultralights, took off from the John White Management Area in western New York. Fifteen miles out, bad weather forced the first group down, and the second turned back.

"The birds have an instinct to remain where they feel safe," Gavin Shire explained. "They want to follow the planes, but then again they want to be where they feel comfortable. Once they make the decision to turn back, it's very hard to do anything about it."

Other problems followed quickly. Upon approach to landing, Steely, a female, became entangled in wing cables and lost part of a foot to the propeller. On December 6, at Canisteo, New York, Chris, a male, lost a wing in a similar accident.

"We discovered that the wing on our ultralights isn't fast enough for the swans," Shire reported. "It was originally used with geese, which fly seven or eight miles an hour slower than the swans. The trumpeters are able to fly in front of the plane, and I can't pull ahead of them. When that happens, there's a danger of them becoming caught in the top wires, which is what happened to Steely and Chris."

Weather conditions remained poor for several days, and the birds were reluctant to fly. To avoid the risk of further injuries, biologists decided to truck the flock the remainder of the migration route, stopping every forty miles and flying the swans at each location in a five-mile radius and to altitudes of one thousand feet in the hope they would learn enough of the topography to permit them to find their way back. The flock arrived at Horsehead by vehicle on December 16 without additional casualties.

Although the swans displayed migration intention behavior, no migration was initiated during the spring of 1999, and the flock was relocated to the Oak Orchard Wildlife Management Area in New York, only a few miles from where they had been trained the previous year. Here they adapted quickly to the wetlands and were monitored several times a week by volunteers.

Two swans died during the summer, one of aspergillosis, a disease caused by mold fungus, and the other was believed to have struck a power line. During the fall hunting season, however, five were illegally shot by hunters, and one died of lead poisoning after ingesting shotgun pellets.

On January 6, 2000, five of the remaining six swans were collected and transported back to the wintering area on Chesapeake Bay. One—identified as R18 by its neck band—was missing. Remarkably, the bird was relocated on January 22 near Claysburg, Pennsylvania, having flown two hundred and ten miles—two-thirds of the migration route back to Maryland. R18 continued to move south and is expected to return to New York in the fall.

New studies have demonstrated that if cygnets are taken from their parents at ten days of age, they will learn to follow an ultralight better than those hatched in an incubator. It is additionally believed that Alaskan trumpeters have a genetic advantage for migration over ones that have bred for several generations in captivity, and therefore the project is seeking permits to collect up to thirty ten-day-old cygnets from Alaska, provide them with initial training at Airlie, then transport them to New York, where they will be trained to follow the ultralights.

And so, through the patience of a group of dedicated biologists, pilots, and volunteers, the grandest of our native waterfowl slowly returns to its historical range—to the lonely coves of Chesapeake Bay, where Lovey Lake once thrilled to the whistle of their wings and their high-pitched, mellow coos.

∞

I was visiting some years ago, and I needed a haircut, so I went into this barber shop. Evidently they had redone a theater, and the barber had taken a row of seats and put half of them on one side of the shop and half on the other, and he had a stove in the middle.

When I went in, all these guys were sitting in there, so I sat down to wait my turn.

Pretty soon the barber said, "Next."

I just sat there because all these people were ahead of me.

Finally he looked at me and said, "You're next." They were all in there just talking.

He started cutting, and he said, "You're new around here, aren't you?"

I said, "Yep."

He waited a while and said, "Do you live here or are you just visiting?"

I said, "Just visiting."

He cut some more, and then he said, "Who?"

I got to the point where if I needed a haircut, and we were

going to come down here in a week or two, I'd wait.

I got a haircut one day, and when I came back up to my mother-in-law's, they started to giggle. I said, "What's so funny?"

They said, "Have you looked in the mirror?"

I said, "No," and I went in to a mirror and took off my glasses. Bill had trimmed my eyebrows, and he cut one completely off. I think he liked a little dandelion wine from time to time.

∞

Ogle Bradford had a store down below named Worlds End. It was right at the top of Worlds End Creek. It was stuck right out in the country—wasn't a single house anywhere near it.

Now this is a true story. My friend Theodore had another fellow huntin' with us one time from over on the western side of the bay, and Theodore decided he wanted to stay over another night. This fellow says, "Well, I'd like to stay with you, but I'll have to call my wife."

So we had to go up to Ogle Bradford's to use his phone. Now this was back in the days when you had party lines, and you could hardly hear anything. You had to shout into that thing. So this fellow was a-shoutin': "Honey, Theodore wants me to spend another night down here!"

She says, "Well, I guess that's O.K. Where are you?

The fellow says, "Theodore, where am I?"

Theodore says, "Worlds End."

The fellow shouts into that mouthpiece, "I'm at Worlds End, honey!"

"Damn," she says, "you're drunk again!"

∞

A Sampler
of Tidewater Tales

The steamboat era on Chesapeake Bay has been called "romantic," but in the nineteenth and early twentieth centuries water travel provided the only practical connection between population centers and vast rural areas sprawling along the estuary and its tributaries. The steamboat was more than a romance; it became a necessity.

To satisfy the critical need of transporting commercial and agricultural products as well as people to and from every navigable corner of Bay Country, fifty or more steamers operated out of Baltimore, and a similar number sailed from Norfolk and Washington.

The history of these smoke-and-fire-belching behemoths includes many exciting tales, some tragic, others of victory against odds. One of the latter occurred on a stormy night in August, 1887, but allow me a few words of background before I tell the story.

In 1883, prompted by the need for additional transport services to the Eastern Shore, Dorchester County residents Eldridge S. Johnson and John W. Woodland pooled their resources and founded The Choptank Steamboat Company. They began operations with a chartered steamer, the William E. Clark, providing night service between Baltimore and landings at Easton, Oxford, Cambridge, and along the Choptank River. The first of three screw steamers built by Johnson and

Woodland, the *Choptank*, was under construction at the time operations began.

On the last Saturday in August, 1887, with storms rumbling across the entire Chesapeake Bay region, *Choptank* slipped her moorings at Baltimore's Light Street Pier and pointed her bow toward the bay and Cambridge. The time was 11:00 p.m.

Captain Charles W. Wright knew that his vessel—sailing at three hundred and forty-six gross tons—could handle rough weather and was certain they would encounter some in the hours ahead. He turned in to secure a little rest before reaching open water.

As *Choptank* passed Fort Carroll, flashes of lightning began to illuminate the horizon. On her bridge the first mate sensed that the bay would soon become a dangerous place for lesser boats.

At the mouth of the Patapsco River the wind mounted in force and intensity. Swells matured into waves, with breakers curling on their crests and crashing over *Choptank*'s superstructure. In their cabins, passengers held on as best they could.

Several miles below Sevenfoot Knoll, the lookout sighted a yacht on his starboard and expressed concern for the small craft's survival. Shortly thereafter his fears were realized when the sail suddenly disappeared.

The lookout reported to the first mate, who summoned the skipper. Captain Wright immediately called for a volunteer crew of oarsmen to man a lifeboat, positioning himself in the stern sheets as the fragile craft was nearly crushed against *Choptank*'s hull by the angry bay.

Applying every muscle in their arms and backs to the task, the drenched oarsmen pulled the dory over looming, froth-capped waves toward the locality where the sail had last been observed, while Captain Wright repeatedly hailed the shipwrecked crew.

Presently a faint reply was returned by the gale, and oarsmen redoubled their efforts when the turbulent night finally surrendered a glimpse of the overturned craft. Through a pummeling wall of rain and salt spray, the rescuers heard an agonized appeal: "For God's sake save the kid!"

By an almost super-human effort on the part of Captain Wright and his volunteers, the entire crew of the ill-fated yacht, four men and a young boy, were pulled into the lifeboat; and finally, with all hands secure on board, *Choptank* proceeded safely through the storm to Cambridge.

And now, as that fellow on the radio would say, "Here's the rest of the story."

In August, 1921, Captain Wright and his daughter boarded a coastal steamer bound for Boston out of Baltimore, under the command of William P. Pratt. Because of his prominence in steamboat circles, Wright was invited to take his meals at the captain's table.

After breakfast had been served on the first morning out, a young lady in the congenial party began to question the ship's master regarding his experiences at sea.

"My career on the water," responded Pratt, "nearly came to an end before it began, when I was only a lad of ten."

"And how was that?" inquired his fair inquisitor, who by now had gained the undivided attention of everyone at the table.

"I was on a yachting trip," continued the captain, "and during a heavy blow late one evening we capsized just below Sevenfoot Knoll. I won't ever forget the terror of that night. While we desperately clung to the sides of our overturned craft, we thought our chances of being saved were remote. But luck was with us, and about midnight we were picked up by a passing bay steamer. That was the closest call I ever had on the water," Pratt concluded.

"That would have been in August, 1887," observed Captain Wright, who had been showing a keen interest in Pratt's story.

"That's right," responded the skipper. "How is it that you happen to know the date?"

"I also know that the steamer which rescued you was the

Choptank," Wright added with a twinkle in his eye.

"I'm astonished," said Pratt, "There are only a few people alive who could be acquainted with the incident."

"I was captain of the *Choptank* in 1887, and I was in the boat that rescued you," Wright modestly announced, "but for all of the years I've known you, I never realized until now that you were the boy on that yacht."

After years of distinguished service as a steamboat master, Captain Wright was appointed to the post of United States Steamboat Inspector in Baltimore and eventually retired from that position.

On March 9, 1894, Choptank Steamboat Company sold out to the Eastern Shore Railroad Company. Under her new owner, *Choptank* continued to ply the waters of the Chesapeake and its tributaries until she was dismantled for salvage in February, 1927.

∞

Wade H. Murphy, Jr., is a third-generation waterman. For most of his life he has dredged for oysters in winter and run crab lines in summer, "But we're in a bad time now," he will tell you, "and it's not gonna come back like it used to be."

Some years ago Murphy bought the *Rebecca T. Ruark*. Built in 1886, she is the oldest operating skipjack on Chesapeake Bay. He refers to her affectionately as "my *Rebecca*," and she has come to provide him with an additional line of work.

"The last six years," Murphy said, "I've been sailin' charter durin' the summer, and I do it in the winter too, whoever's brave enough to come out. You can pay me fifty dollars for a day and help me cull the oysters. You remember what Tom Sawyer said: 'If you give me an apple, you can paint my fence.' Well, that's the way it is with my *Rebecca*." Wade Murphy is proud of his lady and makes no attempt to conceal the fact.

Murphy once encountered his *Rebecca* on a late winter's day in the Choptank River, at a time when she was under the command of another prideful owner. It's Wade's story, so I'll let him tell it:

"It was in March of the '77, '78 season, and I was drudgin' the Choptank River off Benoni Point. I was drudgin' maybe a couple hundred yards from the lighthouse, where it drops off the edge. The first part of the season you go along the top of the hill, but the more the season goes on, the more you got to get around the edge of the bars.

"We put marker buoys overboard when we find a spot. If the wind is from the west or east, we have to tack across. We don't go headwind or fairwind; we go across it.

"It was the last of the season. I was in my old boat then, and she was hard to sail, but I was workin' beautiful, catchin' a lot of oysters. We were happy.

"I looked up the river, and here come my *Rebecca Ruark*. Old man Emerson Todd from Cambridge had her then. He's dead and gone now, but he was still drudgin' then.

"He tried to find some oysters up on top of the hill, but nothin'. He made two or three dips, and I'm still workin' back and forth. Then he went to the lower part, on the mud. On the mud there wasn't nothin'. Then he made a lick by my buoy. Two boats on the drudge now, but there was all the oysters you wanted.

"Well, there's such a thing as workin' together. He was faster, so with the same kind of wind he'll go faster than me. What he should 'a' done: he should 'a' rigged his sail—slowed down—so I could keep up with him. This was my place that I found, and I was workin' it.

"But he didn't do that. He didn't want to work with me; he wanted to take it over. He come by and seen the oysters, and he liked it, and he's gonna stay there.

"So he's comin', and I go in to make my dip. Well, *Rebecca* is a lot bigger than my boat and could sail better. He could outmaneuver me. We got almost to the bar, and he made me keep off. So there I am with nothin', and he went right in there—two bushel a drudge.

"I went out and about, and he went out and about. We come together again, and he made me keep off the second time. He got another load of oysters, and I didn't get nothin'.

"I got five or six men that's workin' for me, and there they are: 'What are you doin'? You gonna let this guy take over?'

"Well, I went in and about, and he went out and about. We come together again, and he made me keep off again.

"All right!

"Next time I went in and about, and we come together. I didn't keep off; I struck him right over top of the cabin and went down his side. We got davies [davits] that hold the yawl boat on the stern, and I knocked one of his davies loose, so his yawl boat was draggin' in the water. The boats were still together at this point—say it was about a ten-mile-an-hour wind and the sea about a foot and a half high. I was so mad I didn't even think about it.

"What you do when two boats run together like this: the boat on the windward side will pull his jib off, and the boat on the lower side will pull his mainsail off, and they'll separate.

"Well, the boats were still together, and I was hollerin', 'Pull your jib off!'

"This old man was seventy-five years old, and I respected him till this, but I was gettin' ready to get on that boat. I said, 'If you don't pull the jib off, I'm gonna pull it off for you!' I'd had my mainsail down, but he had me covered, and it wasn't doin' no good. Finally he took the jib off. She come up, and we fell apart.

"Well, he had to drop his yawl boat down, and he had to go home. He couldn't drudge, and draggin' his yawl boat in the water. So he went to Cambridge, and I went on workin'—had a beautiful sail. Nobody else bothered me, and I caught my limit—a hundred and fifty bushel—by two o'clock.

"The wind was about southeast, and we just sailed on to Tilghman and put my oysters out.

"It was a Friday. We normally run a half a day on Saturday, but the weatherman was callin' for a northwest, and it looked like it was gonna do that. I said, 'OK boys, I'll pay you off this evenin', and we won't work tomorrow 'cause it ain't gonna be fit no way. So I paid 'em off and went home.

"That evenin' I got to thinkin' about it, so I called this old man over in Cambridge. I called him up, and I said, 'Captain Emerson, I'm not workin' tomorrow. You want me to help fix your boat, I'll come over and help you.'

"He said, 'You didn't hurt my boat.'

"I said, 'I didn't hurt your boat? I knocked the davies off of her.'

"He said, 'You fix your boat, and I'll fix mine.'

"I said, 'I didn't hurt mine.'

"He said, 'You didn't hurt mine either.'

"We went back and forth, and I said, 'Well, I'll tell you what: If you want me to come down, I'll help you.'

"He said, 'What did you holler at me for anyway?'

"I said, 'Captain Emerson, you were hoggin' today. We could have both got our limits. There was plenty oysters out there, but you tried to take over. You wouldn't let me get to my own place, and I'll do it again tomorrow if you come around me.'

"That's exactly the way it went down."

∞

In the wintertime I have five, six men that work with me on the boat. Summertime I only have one friend. My dog goes with me every day—used to. He misses some days now. He went with me through the summer eight or ten years, and it got so I could understand what he was sayin'.

I tell these guys that dog talks to me, and they say,

"You're nuts; the dog can't talk."

It made me feel bad, and I said, "Enough. I got to prove it somehow." But anyway, one day that he really talked, when I got back and told 'em, they believed me.

We were workin' in the Choptank River—trotlinin'. When you trotline—I guess a lot of people know—like you establish your own place—your own lay—and you go to the same place every day. Ninety percent of the people respect it, and they don't bother you, but you got to go every day if you want to keep it.

So I'd been workin' on the Dorchester side of the Choptank, the east side of the river, and I'd been doin' real good. Best summer I ever had, catchin' a load of crabs more than other people. I was happy.

I got up this mornin', and it was blowin' a gale northwest, which summertime the prevailing wind is southeast. Wintertime it's northwest. Well, this day in the summer it was from the northwest.

As soon as I got out to the truck, my dog was standin' there. I said, "Well, what do you think, black dog?" And he looked at me and didn't say nothin'. So we got in the truck, went up to the boat, and he jumped out the back and got aboard. He was rarin' to go. It was blowin' a gale and wasn't fit to go, but I said, "Well, I been doin' good. If I don't go across the river, I'm gonna lose my place. You might go up a creek this particular day and do good, and somebody else may go to where you at, and you've lost it. You can't go two places. I said, "Well, OK."

So we started across the river; it's three or four miles across there. The wind was blowin' from the northwest, and we were goin' southeast—fair wind across the river. When I got to where my marker was, I turned my boat around, and the trot line upset right in the bottom of the boat. I looked at the black dog and I said, "Black dog, what do you think now?"

He said, "Ruff, Ruff!"

I said, "Daggone right it's rough."

Those guys never did say no more.

∞

Over here to the island they were drudgin' one day, and they caught a human skeleton.

The captain said, "You get that thing back overboard."

But the crew said, "No, we'll bury it on the land tonight."

Well, they never got in till late that night, and they forgot about it.

Next mornin' the captain got up, and there was that skeleton, and he grabbed it, and he let it go overboard.

Norman said, "Now what did you do that for?"

Captain said, "I don't want nobody aboard here that can't cull oysters."

∞

I've been married to a waterman for thirty-eight years—thirty-eight years to figure this man out. Sometimes he's out on the bay all day tongin', and he makes it sound so romantic. I ain't never seen nothin' romantic about it myself.

Out there he uses one cup, and it's never seen a drop of water in it to wash it—stays stinky the whole year. Out to the bay he looks into that cup and thinks it's the greatest thing ever was, but settin' at the table sometimes—one little piece of somethin' on a fork and, "This fork's dirty." It's hard to figure out.

He's got the best thing at home he ever could have. Luckiest day he ever had was when he got me. So he's got me at home, and then he's got his boat.

He's never heard me say this 'cause I just thought of it, and he's been up in Rock Hall tongin' all week. I just figured it out. It just come to me. I believe the Lord give it to me. He looks at that boat like a mistress. He does. He does! And he takes care of her too.

If she needs a new sail or stern post, he'll take that boat right to the railway. Now what woman wouldn't want a new sail and stern post. Then he gets beadin' goes all the way a-round her. I've never had a necklace from him that went all the way around me. You know, wives like diamonds and ru-bies and emeralds—I do. Well, he can't afford 'em, but it's diamonds and emeralds and rubies for that boat, and they'll shine out over a mile or more in the dark. You call 'em run-nin' lights.

I figured it out, and I really know what it is now. She's a-layin' there, and ain't nobody gonna bother her but him. She ain't a-goin' nowhere; ain't a-goin' to work without him. He gets in that boat, and he can boss her. Any time he wants her to go, she'll go.

A man and his boat is hard to separate.

∞

These sailin' boats came each winter, and I thought I'd like to know somethin' about the people aboard. What the mind knows about this water is one thing, but to know what the heart knows is another, and these people were the heart of the bay.

One of the first men I met was Captain Orville Parks, who won all the skipjack races with the Rosie Parks. When I met him, I said, "I'm from Solomons," real proud.

He said, "I know them doctor fellows down there," and I knew right away that he had a different vision of them than I had.

He said, "I took some of them out on the river, and they dropped a bottle down and got some water up. They took it down in the cabin to measure onto that, and one of them fellas said, 'That water ain't too good, Captain.'

"I said, 'Well maybe it ain't; I don't know.'

"He said, 'We'll pick out some of these oysters.'

"So I dropped the drudge down and got up an oyster or two.

"One fellow took an oyster and shucked it out, and he come up and said, 'Captain, that oyster's got enough poison in it to probably kill two or three men.'

"About that time my mate was gettin' tired of hearin' all of it. He said, 'Give me that darned oyster.' He went 'slurp'—ate it just like that—and he ain't dead yet."

That's a story Captain Orville told to teach me about balance.

∞

The last five stories in this collection were edited from anecdotes told during a watermen's program at the Avalon Theater in Easton, Maryland, by Wade Murphy, Dallas Bradshaw, Janice Marshall, and Tom Wisner.

Down on
de East'n Sho'

Once when the late Miss Nora Foxwell recited a poem for me, I applauded and asked if she had written it.

"Not exactly," she replied. "Everything I see, if it takes my eyes, I put my mind to it and fix it to suit myself."

So when a friend sent me an old, framed poem recently, I took a cue from Miss Nora and fixed it to suit myself. I wish I could give credit to the originator of the somewhat longer and different version, but it was presented anonymously.

Go 'way now Honey, don't yuh know
Dar ain't no place lak' de East'n Sho'!
I tells yuh man, fo' de simple truf,
Dar's whar at, I spen' my youf!
'Way down dar, by de sunny sho',
Why yuh jes' eat, till yuh can't no mo'!
Ebber t'ing good, jes' grow in dat wada,
'An' all de folks eat more'n dey oughta.
Dat's why, Ise tell yuh, dey's big an' strong,
'An' dey all gits fat 'fore dey be dar long.

De land, it am so rich as cream,
An' de fields an' woods in de sun do gleam!
De sky am blue, an' dar ain't no sto'm

When de summer breeze blow wa'm.
De oyster, dey am nice an' la'ge;
De fishes dey come in shoals!
De folks down dar don't live on pig,
Whar de ol' A'lantic rolls!
It's jes lak shoppin' in Hebbin's sto,
Down on de East'n Sho.

∞

Order Hal Roth's books from your favorite bookstore or by mail with a credit card from Washington Book Distributors at 1-800-699-9113.

Conversations in a Country Store—*Reminiscing on Maryland's Eastern Shore* (1995)
Trade Paperback, ISBN 0-9647694-0-9
$12.95 + shipping

You Can't Never Get to Puckum—*Folks and Tales from Delmarva* (1997)
Trade Paperback, ISBN 0-9647694-1-7
$10.95 + shipping

The Monster's Handsome Face—*Patty Cannon in Fiction and Fact* (1998)
Printed Case, ISBN 0-9647694-2-5
$19.95 + shipping

The Entailed Hat by George Alfred Townsend
Edited and Illustrated by Hal Roth (2000)
Trade Paperback, ISBN 0-9647694-3-3
$16.95 + shipping

You Still Can't Get to Puckum—*More Folks and Tales from Delmarva* (2000)
Trade Paperback, ISBN 0-9647694-4-1
$14.95 + shipping